Endorsements

Unity is found in confessing the faith together. But what if interpretations of that confession seem to clash? Hopefully, we talk to each other rather than about each other. That was the goal of the colloquium at the 2014 Synod of the United Reformed Churches in conversation with the Canadian Reformed Churches. Good progress was made. The spirit of this discussion is a model and the substance is of great importance, especially to those who joyfully embrace the Reformed confession.

—Dr. Michael Horton, URC minister and J. Gresham Machen Professor of Theology and Apologetics at Westminster Seminary California

Having recently taught a seminary course on the history of covenant theology in Reformed churches, I found this remarkably open and frank dialogue on the critical doctrine of covenant between able representatives of the United Reformed and Canadian Reformed federations to be enlightening, fascinating, and helpful. There is scarcely any more important doctrine in the Bible than covenant to get right, and yet no other doctrine in the Reformed faith has so many nuanced and distinctive emphases between various Reformed and

Presbyterian denominations—hence the importance and value of having such discussions as these. This book should be read and reflected on by anyone who is serious about understanding the Reformed faith—ministers and church members alike.

>   —Dr. Joel R. Beeke, President and Professor of Systematic Theology and Homiletics, Puritan Reformed Theological Seminary, Grand Rapids, MI

I am particularly thankful for the contributions from Drs. Van Raalte and Van Vliet from the CanRC Seminary, which augurs, in my view, a better day on the part of the CanRC in ecumenical dealings . . . Here's hoping that this dialog, and others like it to come, will bring the URCNA and the CanRC closer, and that the OPC and others of like faith would be drawn closer to them and each other. The times in which we live make it clearer than ever that we can ill afford to remain distant from those of like faith and practice. May the Lord be pleased ever to draw us all closer to Him and in that process closer to each other!

>   —Dr. Alan D. Strange, Professor of Church History, Mid-America Reformed Seminary, Dyer, IN

These churchmen and scholars, all of whom I hold in the highest regard, provide other Reformed Confessional denominations with a valuable guide on how to have thoughtful, frank, and kind-spirited theological discussions about issues of paramount importance. There is so much to learn in this book, not only regarding the content but also the manner in which they dialogue with each other. I honestly believe that Westminsterian denominations (e.g., PCA, OPC) could learn a lot from this book, and it is my hope that similar types of discussions will take place in the future in our own denominations. Ministers from both the

URC and CanRef churches should also read this book in order to be reminded afresh of the appropriate boundaries of Reformed confessional covenant theology.

—Dr. Mark Jones, Minister at Faith PCA, Vancouver, BC

This delightful discussion proves beyond a doubt that any differences between the URC and CanRC federations are differences in history, emphasis and language rather than differences of substance or theology. Heartily recommended!

—Dr. Gerhard H. Visscher, Principal and Professor of New Testament, Canadian Reformed Theological Seminary, Hamilton, ON

The Bond of The

Covenant Within The

Bounds of The

Confessions

The Bond of The Covenant Within The Bounds of The Confessions

A Conversation Between the URCNA and CanRC

Edited by John A. Bouwers and Theodore G. Van Raalte

CHURCH UNITY PUBLICATIONS

St. Catharines, ON

The Bond of The Covenant Within The Bounds of The Confessions
copyright © 2015 by John A. Bouwers

Creative Commons license: You are free to share, copy, and redistribute the material in any medium or format as well as adapt, remix, transform, and build upon the material for any purpose, even commercially. You may do so in any reasonable manner, but not in any way that suggests the licensor endorses you or your use. You must give appropriate credit (editors, title, publication data) and indicate whether changes were made.

Scripture quotations in this work are taken from the NIV and ESV.

Holy Bible, New International Version, NIV. Copyright © 1973, 1978, 1984, 2011 by Biblica, Inc. Used by permission. All rights reserved worldwide.

The Holy Bible, English Standard Version (ESV), copyright © 2001 by Crossway, a publishing ministry of Good News Publishers. Used by permission. All rights reserved.

Publisher's Cataloguing-in-Publication data

The Bond of the Covenant Within The Bounds of The Confessions: A Conversation Between the URCNA and the CanRC / John A. Bouwers and Theodore G. Van Raalte.

xii. 135 p., 23 cm.

Includes Index

ISBN: 978-0-9947963-0-1 (pbk)

ISBN: 978-0-9947963-1-8 (ePub)

1. Covenant theology—Biblical teachings. 2. Covenant theology–History of doctrines. 3. Church–Unity. 4. Christian union. 5. United Reformed Churches of North America. 6. Canadian Reformed Churches. 7. Christian councils and synods

I. Bouwers, John A. II. Van Raalte, Theodore G.

Contents

Acknowledgements		xi
Introduction: California Covenant Conversation JOHN A. BOUWERS		1
1.	Summary of the Doctrine of the Covenants: A URCNA Perspective CORNELIS P. VENEMA AND W. ROBERT GODFREY	13
2.	Summary of the Doctrine of the Covenants: A CanRC Perspective THEODORE G. VAN RAALTE AND JASON P. VAN VLIET	21
3.	Colloquium at Synod Visalia, June 4, 2014 BOUWERS, GODFREY, VAN RAALTE, VAN VLIET, VENEMA	37
4.	Question Period at Synod Visalia June 4, 2014 BOUWERS, GODFREY, VAN RAALTE, VAN VLIET, VENEMA	69
5.	A Common Covenant Theology? Thoughts on the CanRC/URC Colloquium DANIEL R. HYDE	95
6.	Response to Rev. Daniel Hyde's, "A Common Covenant Theology?" THEODORE G. VAN RAALTE AND JASON P. VAN VLIET	103

7. *Postponement or Progress? Personal reflections*   *109*
    on Synod Visalia 2014
    JASON P. VAN VLIET

Appendix 1: Reflections on the Conclusions of Utrecht   *115*
CERCU

Appendix 2: The Conclusions of Utrecht 1905   *123*
SYNOD OF UTRECHT 1905, TRANSLATED BY J. MARK BEACH

Indices   *129*

About the Authors   *135*

Acknowledgements

We sincerely thank the Committee for Ecumenical Relations and Church Unity (CERCU) of the United Reformed Churches (URCNA) for organizing a fruitful meeting between representatives of the United Reformed and Canadian Reformed Churches on the topic of the covenant. Not only did the committee initiate the colloquium that was held at Synod Visalia in California on June 4, 2014, but they also had the participants prepare several months prior by exchanging papers. The committee circulated these to all the members of the Synod and each United Reformed Church in advance. Afterward each Canadian Reformed Church (CanRC) also received copies.

The idea of publishing the proceedings arose already at the Synod. Thanks to Rev. Jordan Huff of the Sunnyside, WA URC who had the presence of mind to record the colloquium. Rev. John Bouwers then set himself to the tedious work of transcribing from an audio recording all of the colloquium and the discussion that followed. After investigating how to get the work published, Rev. Bouwers received an offer from Dr. Ted Van Raalte to assist with the formatting and editing. Our schedules did not permit us to give the work undivided attention, but we're thankful to have completed the work now.

Assistance was received from a pool of volunteers in Rev. Bouwers' congregation for copy editing. We kindly thank André,

Acknowledgements

Cliff, Deanna, Doug, Ernie, Gisele, Ike, Julie, Natasha and Rita. In light of their comments, we slightly polished up the record of the discussions, removing distracting occurrences of "and," "so," "ah," "I think," etc. In some places we added words in square brackets or changed a word for ease of reading. In no place did we change the meaning, nor did we drop any sentence from the proceedings. We are confident that this publication is an accurate record of the colloquium and we hope that the slight editing makes the work more pleasing to the reader.

We also acknowledge the assistance of Jeremy Bout and Josh Schouwstra of Edge Factor, who volunteered their help for the cover design. John Van Dyk of *Christian Renewal* is responsible for the photography. We'd also like to mention Rev. Pim DenHollander and Rev. Clarence Vandervelde, members of the Canadian Reformed Committee for Church Unity (CCU), who have maintained a positive approach at numerous URCNA synods, convinced that the Lord desires his church to be fully united. Finally, our warm thanks for the ready cooperation of all the authors. You can read their contributions in what follows.

We pray that the unity of Christ's church will be promoted by this publication and that whatever gains the Lord has granted may be solidified and built up.

July 10, 2015
John Bouwers and Theodore Van Raalte

Introduction: California Covenant Conversation

John A. Bouwers

Introduction

On a hot summer night in Visalia, California, four men sat down together for a theological conversation, *a colloquium*. The night was June 4, 2014. The discussion took place in the middle of the schedule of the Synod of the United Reformed Churches in North America, in the presence of all of its delegates and before a number of interested guests. The conversation that night focused on the doctrine of the covenants in Scripture. This has always been a hot topic among the Reformed churches, and sadly, a teaching that has been at the center of theological disputes and church schisms throughout the generations.

On this particular evening, however, cooler heads prevailed. To be sure, the discussion was not cold, or cold-hearted, not by any stretch of the imagination. How could it have been, as the dialogue partners engaged one another on that which is most fundamental to the Reformed faith, yes, to the Christian religion—the blessing of our fellowship with the living, Triune God, in Christ! The discussions were calm and careful, but appropriately warm and interesting as the participants engaged

Introduction

one another winsomely and in a brotherly fashion with the Scriptures, and our Reformed Confessions.

The participants in the dialogue were four theological professors who had come to this conversation in California from across North America. Two represented the United Reformed Churches in North America: Dr. Robert Godfrey, president of Westminster Seminary in California; and Dr. Cornel Venema, president of Mid-America Reformed Seminary. The other two came from Hamilton, ON, Canada: Dr. Ted Van Raalte and Dr. Jason Van Vliet, both professors of the Canadian Reformed Theological Seminary.

In the context of the ongoing merger discussions between the Canadian Reformed Churches and the United Reformed Churches, the challenge for the evening was to seek to give an answer to this question, "Given our common confessions, is there a mutual understanding and agreement between our federations on the doctrine of the covenant? In a warm, congenial and fraternal manner, the discussion partners were able, not superficially, but seriously and honestly, to engage the issues. Helpful injections of humour demonstrated their mutual respect and appreciation for one another as brothers. The end-result was a blessing both in its clarifying of the issues and in the way it helped to remove a deterrent in the ongoing challenge to pursue more complete unity. The upshot of the discussion was that the colloquium participants, as careful scholars and respected leaders and churchmen in our respective federations, could together conclude, based on their discussion, that despite differing historical developments and the resulting variations with regard to the way the doctrines of the covenants are taught in our respective churches, we can nevertheless find each other within the bounds of the confessions. For whatever differences of expression on the matter, we are confessionally united.

The Background

The United Reformed Churches and the Canadian Reformed Churches have been in a Phase 2—*Ecclesiastical Fellowship* relationship as sister churches since the decisions of their respective synods (Neerlandia and Escondido) in 2001. The hope and expressed commitment of the churches when entering into such a sister-church relationship has always been that, should the Lord in his grace bless and prosper our efforts as churches, the ideal would be that one day full merger or organic union would come to pass, making the two bodies one. Since the 2001 decisions, the Lord has blessed and prospered the relationship between our churches, especially in Canada where our respective churches, being in close proximity to each another, have come to know and appreciate each other more and more. On the broader level, however, our relationship has not been without its challenges. We have been learning over the years that this is a relationship that needs the Lord's blessing and must not be pursued lightly, superficially or hastily.

Our challenges and failings notwithstanding, our federations have, as a whole, sought to be faithful to our scriptural calling and synodical mandate to work "toward complete church unity." The two most recent URC Synods have committed the churches "to continue to engage the issue of an eventual merger between the CanRC and the URC." Most of the progress has been made where our respective churches are in close geographical proximity. Growing love, mutual knowledge and trust, as well as increased cooperation in such things as education, evangelism, youth activities, conferences, joint services, and pulpit exchanges have marked the past number of years. It is significant that the closer and more frequent the interaction has been, the greater is the interest and openness toward pressing onward in this endeavor.

The Challenges

From our observations and experience, we would characterize three types of concerns that have developed and persisted to deter the prospect of full unity between these two federations. The first is theological, pertaining to the doctrine of the covenants. The second has to do with church polity. Given negative past experiences with hierarchicalism, there are continued fears concerning perceived hierarchical tendencies in the Proposed Joint Church Order. The third has to do with the will to ecumenism generally; some are not convinced that churches that share a confession are required to seek organizational unity. In our discussions we came to the conclusion that if the first two types of objections could be addressed to our mutual satisfaction, many of the hesitations with regards to the third could also be alleviated.

The intent in preparing for the colloquium that took place was to begin by addressing the fundamental, foundational doctrinal matter, namely the doctrine of the covenants. With the appearance on the North American scene of the *Federal Vision* movement, and with the response to these developments by the United Reformed Churches in the way of *Pastoral Advice* (Synod Schererville, 2007) and *Doctrinal Affirmations* (Synod London, 2010), the perception has arisen among some that the Canadian Reformed Churches are more tolerant of *Federal Vision* teachings than are the United Reformed. At the same time the Canadian Reformed, given their own experiences, historically, with *the Liberation* of 1944, have expressed their own apprehensions, particularly in terms of their general aversion to what they perceive as the danger of making extra-confessional statements. Is it possible that in our respective concerns over against each other, that we have ended up speaking past each other, and missing each other? Certainly, if there is to be ecumenical progress between us, we would need to be convinced as churches that the doctrine of the covenant taught in our respective churches can live healthily side by side in one federation within the bounds of our confessions.

The Colloquium: A Conversation Proposed

In order that we might seek to face the challenge directly and thoroughly, it was decided to organize a public discussion to be held in the context of a URC Synod. Four men were assembled for the task, all of whom were at the same time reputable scholars and respected churchmen. In preparation for the colloquium, each pair of men was asked to interact with the other pair in an effort to come to an agreement concerning the matters of potential concern that would need to be addressed. Papers and responses were then prepared (they are appended in the following chapters of this publication). These papers were then distributed to the Consistories of the churches, for the URC consistories this was done in preparation for the URC Synod. With this information in hand, the delegates could be prepared to profit from the conversation that would take place between the four men, as they discussed their conclusions, concerns and interacted with one another publicly before the delegates.

The original intent was that all of this would take place in the space of an hour of the synod's time. In God's gracious providence, the synodical delegates graciously and wisely determined to set aside a whole evening session for the discussion, one hour for the discussion among the participants, and a subsequent, additional hour for discussion and interaction with the synodical delegates from the floor. The hope and expectation was that such a discussion would promote greater confidence in our mutual adherence to our Confessions. The participants, it will be appreciated, are men of eminent qualification and ability, as well as of integrity. They were not asked to participate in a sort-of sell-job for unity. They all understood very clearly that they would serve the Lord and the churches best with a clear articulation and engagement of the concerns that would need to be addressed. We believe that by interacting in the way they did, they helped the churches both better understand the issues and be more convinced of the confessional unity enjoyed between our federations.

The Fruitful Contribution

A word is in order regarding the contributions of the participants.

Dr. Venema, with his breadth of knowledge and experience in the field of Reformed dogmatics served the colloquium very well, both in getting the discussion going as well as in having it focused on the areas of greatest potential challenge. We would not have been helped by skirting the challenges. Dr. Venema's appreciation, Bavinck-like, for something of the historical Reformed consensus on the matters that most needed to be discussed among us, provided the indispensable foundation that enabled a discussion of considerable substance and profit to take place.

Dr. Godfrey, together with his injection of a number of humorous, sometimes graciously self-deprecating comments, was also able to make a contribution that was extremely significant. His remarks regarding the URC being the more *presbyterianized* over against the Canadian Reformed who have not experienced as much of that influence, were very trenchant and will continue to serve us in our understanding of each other and in the way forward. It was particularly helpful that these remarks of Dr. Godfrey were made in the context of his recognition of and deepened appreciation for the confessional unity that exists between us and the Canadian Reformed Churches. Dr. Godfrey's expressed challenges to the Canadian Reformed brothers in the three areas of (a) objectivity vs. subjectivity, (b) communal vs. personal, and (c) ecclesiastical exclusivity, were helpfully pithy and focused the dialogue profitably. Once again, his periodic injections of humor also helped us to be comfortable with each other and contributed wonderfully to the fraternal spirit we enjoyed together.

Dr. Van Vliet and Dr. Van Raalte are to be thanked for their patient willingness to be placed on the hot seat in the midst of the URC synodical assembly, to face the difficult questions, and even for the way in which they could face challenging anecdotal questions that were later directed to them from the floor. Their kind, gracious, thorough, and helpful answers modeled a spirit of Christ-likeness that was an encouragement to all of us, set an excellent tone for the colloquium and exemplified the grace we all continue to require going forward.

Dr. Van Vliet began his verbal presentation by pointing to Abraham's awe in Genesis 15:12, when God made covenant with him. God's grace to us in his covenant should fill us with a deep sense of awe! Dr. Van Vliet's patient, thorough instruction was flavoured with down-to-earth and fruitful analogies. Most helpful of all were his frequent references to Scripture, to our Confessions and even to our tertiary standards, the liturgical forms.

Dr. Van Raalte's use of Scripture, Confessions, and our liturgical forms was equally prominent and helpful. The particular portion of the pre-synod write-up that has proved very helpful was where he wrote: "We agree that in the decisive matter of the believer's justification, law and gospel are antithetical concepts." What has also served the advancement of our discussion quite noticeably has been Dr. Van Raalte's familiarity and comfort with the developments of Reformed

> We agree that in the decisive matter of the believer's justification, law and gospel are antithetical concepts.

theology in the Scholastic period of the Reformed Orthodox. We trust that Dr. Van Raalte's interest and expertise in this area will continue both to serve the Canadian Reformed Churches as well as our developing relationship, ecumenically. Finally, Dr. Van Raalte's words at the closing of the colloquium evening directing us to Christ from John 12:21—"Sir, we would see Jesus"—gloriously brought our discussion full circle and left us with the focus where it should be, on our faithful Savior.

We want to express our hearty thanks to each of the colloquium participants for their scholarship, for their collegiality and for their love for the gospel and the well-being of the churches. We believe it was a useful and very profitable exercise and was one that enjoyed the rich blessing of God. It is our prayer that the progress we've made may be built upon.

The Outcome

So what was accomplished?

Much in every way. The participants were able to conclude that in spite of our historical differences and varieties of expression (and there are varieties of expression within each federation as well), we do nevertheless find each other's positions within confessional bounds. This means we have, and ought to enjoy, fundamental confessional unity.

This is a far reaching conclusion that must not be overlooked or forgotten. The universal response communicated to us subsequent to the colloquium, by both ecumenical enthusiast and skeptic alike, was that the colloquium was a resounding success, a seriously helpful contribution and a tremendous blessing. We ought to rejoice in it. We need to hold each other to it. We need to stand upon it and live out of it. Ecumenically speaking, as we live up to and out of our confession, we can see that we have a place to stand and a place from which to move forward, in God's good time.

Dr. Alan Strange, the Orthodox Presbyterian ecumenical delegate to synod (who was therefore completely unbiased, being neither United Reformed nor Canadian Reformed) remarked to several of us afterward, that the Holy Spirit's blessing on the colloquium compelled him to say that that day was his best personal experience at an ecclesiastical assembly, ever. The lesson, of course is that as we wait for, pray for, and look for the Spirit's blessing, not forcing the issue, but thoroughly working matters through, we can anticipate even more fruitful progress, with the Lord's blessing in the Lord's time.

All of which helps to put into perspective the "one ecumenical step backward" (if we should even call it that) that Synod took the very next morning after we took "three steps forward" at the colloquium itself. In actual fact it wasn't a step backward at all, it was simply no-step, or a not-yet step, an expression of the churches' desire to catch our breath. The vote "to postpone indefinitely" the motion to encourage CERCU (Committee for Ecumenical Relations and Church Unity of the URC) to come with a proposal to move to the next phase of unity with the Canadian Reformed—Development of a Plan of Union, Phase 3a, was done conscientiously, as the mover of the motion to postpone explicitly expressed, out of a concern not to want to say "no" to such a motion. It was not a "no" but a "not yet."

What the colloquium, and particularly some of the follow-up discussion afterward, made clear was that, now that we have enjoyed the success of the colloquium on the foundational questions, we might consider facing some of the other outstanding practical questions with the same approach in the days and years to come.

The Reporting

In the chapters that follow we will present the opening written contribution of the URC professors (Chapter 1) followed by the

Introduction

contribution and response of the Canadian Reformed professors (Chapter 2). In the next chapter (Chapter 3) we present a transcript of the conversation itself between the four professors, and that is followed by the transcript of the Q&A and discussion period that followed at the Synod (Chapter 4). Chapter 5 is the piece written by URC minister Rev. Daniel Hyde subsequent to the Synod, and printed in *Christian Renewal* wherein he interacts appreciatively with the Canadian Reformed professors and follows up with certain questions. The response of the professors to Rev. Hyde is included next (Chapter 6). Some post synodical reflections of Dr. Van Vliet are included in Chapter 7.

In Appendix 1 we have included the document that was prepared in dialogue with the Interchurch Relations Committee of the Free Reformed Churches and submitted to our respective synods. This document interacts with and reflects upon the *Conclusions of Utrecht* (a decision of the Reformed Churches in the Netherlands in 1905). Our committee has done so in an effort to give expression to the Free Reformed Churches of how the United Reformed Churches see these matters. It is also clear that the Conclusions of Utrecht have no confessional standing among the United Reformed Churches. The relevance of the inclusion of this material (as well as the *Conclusions* themselves in an Appendix 2) with regard to this discussion is that the matters of covenant and its application or appropriation have always been a significant part of our ecumenical discussions with sister-Reformed bodies. Furthermore, our answers to the Free Reformed over against concerns about the error of "presumptive regeneration" flesh out and inform the concerns we have expressed in dialogue with the Canadian Reformed.

What is particularly noteworthy and, we would say, encouraging, is how in the course of our ecumenical dialogue as confessionally Reformed bodies on these matters, there appears to be a growing consensus about the precious teaching of God's covenant and how that blessing is to be experienced and enjoyed among God's people by grace through faith.

Rev. John A. Bouwers

Chairman of the Committee for Ecumenical Relations and Church Unity, URCNA

1

Summary of the Doctrine of the Covenants: A URCNA Perspective

CORNELIS P. VENEMA AND W. ROBERT GODFREY

Introduction

We have been asked by the Committee for Ecumenical Relations and Church Unity (CERCU) of the United Reformed Churches (URCNA) to address the question whether our federations (URCNA and CanRCs) hold to different views of the doctrine of the covenant, and whether these views, though different, fit within the boundaries of acceptable teaching, as these boundaries are defined by the Three Forms of Unity. In order to fulfill this mandate, we decided to focus upon two doctrinal matters: 1) the doctrine of the pre-fall covenant relationship between God and the human race in Adam (commonly termed the "covenant of works"); and 2) the doctrine of the covenant of grace, particularly in respect to its relationship to the doctrine of

> whether these views ... fit within the boundaries of ... the Three Forms of Unity

election. We believe that these are the two primary topics where there may be differences between our two federations.

It should be observed that we do not intend to offer a summary in what follows that fully expresses the diversity of opinion that obtains within the URCNA. What we present is a summary of what we believe is a common understanding of these topics within the URCNA. The key questions are: Are these opinions in conformity to, or within the boundaries set by, the Three Forms of Unity? Are they opinions that the CanRCs believe are within confessional boundaries?

The Pre-fall Covenant ("covenant of works")

We believe that the following theses summarize a common view of the pre-fall covenant, which is held by many in the URCNA to conform to the teaching of the Three Forms of Unity:

1. Adam's obedience to the requirements of his pre-fall fellowship with the Triune Creator was the "condition" for his continuance in and entrance into further life in blessed fellowship with God. The "life" implicitly promised (indeed, the promise of "eternal life" in immutable fellowship with God; cf. Gen. 3:22) in this fellowship would not be a "free gift" of God's saving grace, but a covenanted reward granted in the way of (and in no other way) of Adam's "perfect obedience." What Adam would have received from his Triune Creator, were he to have obeyed the requirements of the pre-fall covenant, would fully accord with divine truth and justice. (See Belgic Confession, Article 14, the "commandment of life"; HC Lord's Day 3.6, "so that [aus dass] he might live with Him in eternal blessedness"; HC Lord's Day 16.40.)

2. Adam's "justification" prior to the fall, though a matter of his "reputation" by God's declaration (forensic), was not on account of the righteousness of Another, but

on account of a righteousness which was his own (though his by virtue of God's favor, enablement and provision). Prior to the fall into sin, Adam was properly reckoned to be righteous by God, but this was not an act of God's saving grace in Christ (see Rom. 5:12-21). Even if Adam's enjoyment of justification and eternal life would not be "merited" by "strict justice" (because it depended upon God's covenanted promise to grant him life on condition of his obedience), it would be granted him as a reward for his obedience. In this respect, it would be a "covenanted merit" or reward based upon Adam's obedience to the condition of the covenant.

3. The justice and truth of God satisfied through the work of Christ, the second Adam, consists in His active and passive obedience. For this reason, we speak (and the confessions consistently speak) of Christ's "merits" or of His "meriting" for us righteousness, favor and eternal life. (See, for example, Belgic Confession, Article 20-23; Heidelberg Catechism, Lord's Days 2-7, 16.40, 23-24.)

4. The Reformed tradition (including Calvin) has always fully concurred with the "distinction" (yes, even a repugnance) between "law" and "gospel," when it comes to the decisive matter of the believer's free justification. (See Belgic Confession, Article 22-23; Heidelberg Catechism, Lord's Days 2,21,23-24,44; Calvin Comm. Jn. 1:17; Rom. 4:15; Gal. 3:19; 2 Cor. 3:6; Deut. 7:9; Institutes II.ix.4; II.7.16; Bavinck, GD, vol. 3, par. 349: "wettisch [and not an] Evangelisch verbond.")

5. The Reformed objection to Rome is not that it uses the language of "merit," but that it speaks of the believer's "merit" rather than acknowledging the perfection, the sufficiency and the power of the merit of Christ imputed to us for justification.

6. Thus, everything that constitutes a necessary and

sufficient basis for affirming a pre-fall covenant of works in distinction from a post-fall covenant of grace is set forth in the Three Forms of Unity. (See, for example, Belgic Confession, Articles 14,20,22,23,24; Heidelberg Catechism, Lord's Days 3-6,15-17,23-24; Canons of Dort Head of Doctrine II; III.2.)

The Covenant of Grace

In the following summary, we begin with points (#1-3) where there is little or no difference of expression or emphasis, so far as we can determine, between our two federations. The following points (#4-6) address areas where there may be differences of expression or emphasis.

    1. After the fall into sin through the disobedience of Adam, the triune Redeemer instituted a second covenant, the covenant of grace, between Himself and believers and their seed. In the covenant of grace, believers are promised salvation and new life through the work of Jesus Christ, the Mediator of the covenant, and are called to faith and obliged unto new obedience.

    2. In the historical administration of the covenant of grace, we may distinguish without separating between the "promises" of the covenant and the "demands" or obligations of the covenant. When believers and their children embrace the covenant promises in Christ in the way of faith, they enjoy the "blessings" of the covenant—fellowship with the living God through Christ and by His indwelling Spirit, the forgiveness of sins and free justification, the restoration of the image of God, renewal in righteousness by the Spirit, and the promise of everlasting life. When believers and their children do not believe or embrace the covenant promises, or walk in a manner that

is consistent with the covenant's demands, they break the covenant and come under God's judgment.

3. Believers and their children may be assured of God's gracious promise to them, which is communicated through Word and sacrament, and be confident in the reliable Word that God speaks to them. The doctrine of election is one that honors God alone as the Savior of His people, and provides a sure basis for the believer's confidence in God's saving power. However, the doctrine of election must be handled with appropriate care, and never be treated in a way that undermines the believer's confidence in God's covenant Word or promise.

4. It is important to distinguish the covenant of grace in its historical administration and the covenant of grace in its saving efficacy (sometimes called the "dual aspect" of the covenant). In its substance and saving efficacy, the covenant of grace is the means whereby God saves his elect people in Christ. Redemption is ultimately a divine gift and gracious inheritance granted in Christ to fallen but elect sinners. The covenant of grace, so far as its saving efficacy is concerned, is not merely a "conditional offer" of salvation to those who are "under" the covenant, but it is also the instrument whereby God communicates to his elect people all that is granted them in Christ. With respect to the saving efficacy of the covenant of grace, God grants to the elect all that is theirs in Christ. The very "conditions" that God stipulates in the covenant of grace, are obtained and granted to the elect upon the basis of the perfect work of Christ on their behalf. (See Canons of Dort, II.8; II, Rejection of Errors 3-6.)

5. The covenant of grace, though it graciously realizes what was typified by the covenant of works, is properly viewed as a "second covenant," and not simply as a re-

institution of the covenant relationship. Because Christ, the Mediator of the covenant of grace, accomplishes all that is necessary for the redemption of His people, and communicates the promise effectually to them by His Spirit, we may not view the promises and demands of the covenant of grace as formally the same as the promises and demands of the covenant of works. Christ gives to His own what He requires of them in the covenant of grace.[1]

6. Though the Three Forms of Unity do not expressly speak of the "visible" and "invisible" church, they do distinguish between those who are "externally" in the church but not genuinely members of Christ (Belgic Confession, Art. 29). The distinction between the covenant in its historical administration and the covenant in its saving efficacy, is parallel to the distinction between all believers and their children who are members of the visible church, and the elect who are known to God (2 Tim. 2:19) and who are properly and genuinely members of Christ and partakers in His saving work. This distinction is an important one to maintain, and is supported by the apostle Paul's distinction between those who enjoy certain covenant

---

1. See F. Turretin, Institutes of Elenctic Theology, Twelfth Topic, Q. 4, #7, 2:191-92. "Nor can it be objected here that faith was required also in the first covenant and works are not excluded in the second . . . They stand in a far different relation. For in the first covenant, faith was required as a work and a part of the inherent righteousness to which life was promised. But in the second, it is demanded—not as a work on account of which life is given, but as a mere instrument apprehending the righteousness of Christ (on account of which alone salvation is granted to us). In the one, faith was a theological virtue from the strength of nature, terminating on God, the Creator; in the other, faith is an evangelical condition after the manner of supernatural grace, terminating on God, the Redeemer. As to works, they were required in the first as an antecedent condition by way of a cause for acquiring life; but in the second, they are only the subsequent condition as the fruit and effect of the life already acquired."

privileges but are not, strictly speaking, "children of the promise" in the sense of God's purpose of election (Rom. 9:6-8).

Note: Regarding the distinction between the "visible" and "invisible" church, we believe that Article 29 of the Belgic Confession is translated properly in the English translation in use in the URCNA. In this translation, the third paragraph reads: "With respect to those who are members of the church, they may be known by the marks of Christians: namely, by faith, and when, having received Jesus Christ the only Savior . . ." In the English translation of this Article in the Book of Praise of the CaRCs, the third paragraph omits the "when" of the original French and Latin (it reads: "Those who are of the church may be recognized by the marks of Christians. They believe in Jesus Christ the only Saviour . . ."). Omitting the "when" of the original may suggest a rather different view as to who genuinely belongs to and is of the church of Jesus Christ.

2

Summary of the Doctrine of the Covenants: A CanRC Perspective

Theodore G. Van Raalte and Jason P. Van Vliet

Introduction

We have been asked by the CERCU of the URCNA and the CCU of the CanRC to address the question whether our respective federations hold different views of the doctrine of the covenant, and whether these views, though possibly different, fit within the bounds of the Three Forms of Unity (TFU).

To the best of our knowledge, we do not believe that any differences between our federations on the topics of covenant and election are of such a nature that they are beyond the bounds of the TFU and therefore doctrinally suspect. In fact, many of the differences *between us* as federations may well also be differences *within* each of our respective federations. Thus, we

> many of the differences *between us* as federations may well also be differences *within* each of our respective federations

have not significantly disagreed with our URCNA brothers Venema and Godfrey, but have pointed out some nuances and further considerations.

We consider it important to note that our CanRC forbears often emphasized that there was no unique "CanRC doctrine/theology/view of the covenant." They were adamant that they were bound simply by what is found in the TFU and that the churches ought to have a measure of flexibility within those bounds.

In addition, it appears to us that the view of the covenant presented by brs. Godfrey & Venema is substantially the same as that which is presented in the Westminster Standards. Since 2001 the CanRCs have had ecclesiastical fellowship (sister church relationship) with the Orthodox Presbyterian Church (OPC), which obviously subscribes to the Westminster Standards. Although the doctrine of the covenant was certainly discussed by the OPC and CanRCs in the years prior to 1998, in the end those discussions did not prevent the relationship of ecclesiastical fellowship from being established. This official decision of Synod Fergus 1998, which has also been upheld and reconfirmed at every CanRC synod since then, indicates that the CanRCs are willing to work with those who hold a Westminster view of covenant theology, without themselves subscribing to the Westminster standards. By the same token, the OPC have not officially objected to any covenant views found within the CanRCs on the basis of their secondary standards. Keeping this broader perspective in mind gives us good hope that the URCNA and CanRCs, both subscribing to the TFU, should be able to find common ground on the doctrine of the covenant.

Finally, we note that the contribution we hereby offer has no official standing in the CanRCs. CERCU and the URCNA Synod will be well aware of the reticence of the CanRCs to adopt position papers and can no doubt appreciate that we are expressing our own views in ways that we think would be helpful for the promotion of unity between the URCNA and the CanRCs.

The considerations below have been crafted in response to questions posed by Drs Godfrey and Venema in an email dated Feb 19, 2014, as well as the summary they have put forward (see "Summary of the Doctrine of the Covenants: A URCNA Perspective"). Thus, our considerations should be understood in that context and not regarded as a comprehensive treatment of the covenant, either pre-fall or post-fall.

Their initial questions were:

(1) What is the understanding of our respective federations regarding the nature of the pre-fall relationship (or covenant) between God, the Triune Creator, and mankind as represented by Adam? We have attached a short summary of what we believe is a common understanding of this pre-fall relationship within the URCNA (see attachment), and would invite you to comment on it from the perspective of the CanRC's.

(2) What is the understanding of our respective federations regarding the nature of the post-fall covenant of grace? We are especially interested in the question of the relation between the formulation of the doctrine of the covenant, with its "promises" and "demands" (conditions? In what sense?), and the doctrine of election. In the URCNA, it is common to speak of the "dual aspect" of the covenant (G. Vos), and to recognize that the conditions of the covenant are ultimately fulfilled in accordance with God's "purpose of election" (Rom. 9:1ff.).

(3) How do the CanRCs regard the decisions of recent URCNA synods—re the doctrine of justification, the federal vision controversy, and the relation between covenant and election? The question is not so much whether the URCNA has (arguably) adopted some form of "extra-confessional binding." Rather, the question focuses upon whether it is permissible, even necessary, to distinguish between the covenant in its historical

administration and the covenant in its substance and efficacy in the salvation of the elect (what is often called the "dual-aspect" of the covenant, or what is expressed by the distinction between the "visible" and "invisible" church).

(4) In the URCNA, it is commonly believed that Article 29 of the Belgic Confession warrants a distinction between those who truly belong to Christ and his church and those who are "externally" members of the (visible) church. This Article is thought to warrant a distinction like that between the "visible" and "invisible" church, or the distinction between those who are "in" but not "of" the covenant people of God. What is the understanding of the CanRC's re this distinction?

> Note: We are curious that the English translation of the Article in the Book of Praise, third paragraph, reads: "Those who are of the church may be recognized by the marks of Christians. They believe in Jesus Christ the only Saviour . . ." In our translation, it reads: "With respect to those who are members of the church, they may be known by the marks of Christians; namely, by faith, and when, having received Jesus Christ the only Savior . . ." Your translation seems to ignore the "when" of the original French and Latin, and may suggest a rather different view as to who genuinely belongs to and is of the church of Jesus Christ.

Thus far the initial questions from Drs. Godfrey and Venema.

Key Considerations concerning the Covenant before the Fall

Concerning Question 1 and Theses on the Pre-fall Covenant

1. We agree that God's covenanted reward of "immutable fellowship" would be given in Paradise by way of Adam's perfect obedience. We agree that Adam was created with the freedom of choice to serve God or not, a freedom he had to exercise rightly,

so that he would show in act and fact that he truly loved his God by submitting to his authority and fulfilling the God-given mandates. However, we point out several nuances:

    a. When God said that his creation was "very good" (Gen 1:31) and when he walked in the cool of the day with Adam and Eve in the Garden *pre-lapsum* (inferred from Gen 3:8) they enjoyed a sinless and uninhibited fellowship with God. Therefore their entrance into "further life" should not be understood to be more than the entrance into a state of *non posse peccare*, or of "immutable fellowship with God" and whatever that entailed. In other words, Adam and Eve already enjoyed the gift of life with God and we should not speak of them as though they lacked any gift or capacity from God, lest we impinge upon created goodness.[1]

    b. When God threatened the sentence of death in the very day that Adam took of the fruit of the tree of the knowledge of good and evil (Gen 2:17), he thereby taught Adam that he had within him the possibility of sinning against God and his neighbour, depending upon the choice of his will. This text, more than Genesis 3:22, ought to be the ground for speaking of Adam's state of *posse peccare*. The history of redemption and history of revelation teach us of God's purpose to bring man to the state of *non posse peccare* (e.g., Rev 21-22).

    c. When Adam obeyed God he did so out of a heart of trust in God. His calling was to have that faith in God which took God at his Word, that hope which looked in faith to the time of "immutable fellowship," and that love

---

1. Editor's note: *pre-lapsum* means "before the fall"; *posse peccare* means "able to sin"; *non posse non peccare* means "not able not to sin"; *posse non peccare* means "able not to sin"; and *non posse peccare* means "not able to sin." These distinctions describe the states of creation, fall, redemption, and consummation in terms that go back at least to Augustine.

which flowed out of such faith. In other words, while the leading measure of Adam's faithfulness was his "personal, perpetual, and perfect obedience" (WCF 7.2, WLC 20), this loving obedience could only have been present together with faith and hope, and particularly as the fruit of such faith/trust. The Westminster Confession thus uses not only "covenant of works" but also "covenant of life" and indeed theologians of the period also spoke of a "covenant of friendship," "legal covenant," "first covenant," and "covenant of nature."

d. We caution against stringing together phrases from the Heidelberg Catechism and the Belgic Confession without due attention to their context, as is done in thesis 1. To wit, the result clause in HC, LD 3.8 "so that he might . . . live with him in eternal blessedness" is not in the context of Adam doing good works but in the context of having been created good – "God created man good and in his image, that is, in true righteousness and holiness, so that . . ." The fuller quotation emphasizes that Adam was created in true righteousness, not that he had to earn it.

e. In sum, the life implicitly promised would be a covenanted reward granted in the way of Adam's perfect obedience. As a covenanted reward, it would still be a gift out of God's favour to the creature. Adam's prefall obedience should be understood to be the leading measure of his trust in God.

2. We affirm that Adam's righteousness or "justification" prior to the fall was a righteousness of his own, though our typical use of the word "justification" applies it to our post-fall forensic justification in Christ. The reward granted to Adam prior to the fall would indeed have been a reward for his obedience within the terms of his relationship with God, that is, a *meritum ex pacto* that consists in claiming the promises that God is already holding out.

In our view, Adam could not have merited his reward by strict justice outside of any covenant terms because that would require the creature to produce something entirely of his own (*ex nihilo*, as it were). But everything, including the terms of Adam's pre-fall relationship with God, is a gift of God (1 Cor 4:7).[2]

Turretin writes, "From these [foregoing considerations] we readily gather that there now can be no merit in man with God by works whatsoever, either of congruity or of condignity . . . Hence it also appears that there is no merit properly so called of man before God, in whatever state he is placed. Thus Adam himself, if he had persevered, would not have merited life in strict justice, although (through a certain condescension [*synchatabasin*]) God promised him by a covenant life under the condition of perfect obedience . . ."[3]

3. We agree wholeheartedly with Godfrey & Venema's thesis. Our confessions clearly teach that Christ alone fully merited our salvation and that God imputes to his elect both the active and passive obedience of Christ.

    a. Although the debate generated by Piscator about the imputation of the active obedience of Christ was subsequent to the composition of the BC and HC we affirm that these should be understood to affirm the doctrine, on the grounds that the *textus receptus* of the BC, as improved by the Synod of Dort 1618-1619, clearly affirms the doctrine in Article 22, "he imputes to us all his merits and as many holy works as he has done for us and in our place."[4] We note also the closing of HC 23.60, "He grants these to me . . . as if I

---

2. Editor's note: *meritum ex pacto* means "merit by virtue of the covenant"; *ex nihilo* means "out of nothing."

3. Francis Turretin, *Institutes of Elenctic Theology*, transl. George M. Giger, ed. James T. Dennison (Phillipsburg: P&R, 1994), vol. 2, p. 712; also quoted in URCNA *Report of the Synodical Study Committee on the Federal Vision and Justification*, footnote 52.

myself had accomplished all the obedience which Christ has rendered for me." Our Form for Lord's Supper celebration also includes, "By his perfect obedience he has for us fulfilled all the righteousness of God's law."

b. At the same time we caution against pressing the term "passive obedience" too far, for it does not mean that Christ was not active in pursuing the cross for our sakes, but that he *suffered* for us as the Paschal Lamb. In this case the word "passive" should be understood according to its shared root with the word "passion," as in the "passion [=suffering] and death" of Christ.

4. We agree that in the decisive matter of the believer's justification, law and gospel are antithetical concepts. Indeed, to affirm this is fundamental to our salvation, as the various confessional references in this thesis affirm (see further our comments on the role of faith in justification below under Covenant of Grace, Consideration 7). Yet we also affirm that in the language of Scripture the gospel is to be "obeyed" and even includes threats (John 3:36, Rev 3:14-22, 2 Thess 1:8, Latin & French of CD 5.14). Scripture thus also speaks of the "law of Christ" (Gal 6:2; 1 Cor 9:21). Scripture teaches us, too, that the law or Torah is a wonderful instruction of the LORD that is full of promises (Psa 119, Eph 6:2-3). Thus, we caution against an arbitrary dichotomization of Scripture texts containing commands into "law" and those containing promises into "gospel."

5. We wholeheartedly agree that we may use the language of merit for Christ's work. We humbly and earnestly confess that Christ has merited our entire salvation. He is our only Saviour, given by grace alone and to be received by faith alone.

6. Venema and Godfrey have affirmed that "everything that

4. Editor's note: *textus receptus* means "received text" in the sense of what has been authoritatively adopted and received by the churches.

constitutes *a necessary and sufficient* basis for affirming a pre-fall covenant of works in distinction from a post-fall covenant of grace is set forth in the Three Forms of Unity." This would seem to imply that all confessors of the TFU *must* affirm the distinction and perhaps also the terms "covenant of works" and "covenant of grace."

On the one hand, we agree in affirming the distinction and disjunction between the pre-fall and post-fall situations. Indeed, we affirm a radical discontinuity that must be strongly emphasized so as to avoid Pelagian errors. Without doubt the fellowship in Paradise could not be restored by man himself; it was done and gone *unless* it was restored through Another, a Mediator, and by faith in him. Adam and Eve died spiritually "on that day," and were thrust permanently from the fellowship in body and soul that they enjoyed with God in the Garden. That fellowship will not be restored fully until our Lord Jesus Christ returns in glory to bring in the new creation.

On the other hand, we do not hold each other to the term "covenant of works," since the TFU do not require the term. We note that the Westminster Standards also use "covenant of life" (WLC, 20) and speak of the covenants of works and grace as "commonly called" (WLC, 30), implying that other terms are possible. Indeed Reformed theologians have affirmed the radical discontinuity between the pre- and post-fall situations by using other terms for the first covenant such as the covenant of nature or creation (Ursinus), covenant of friendship (Burgess, Ball), legal covenant (Sedgwick), covenant of innocence (Henry), covenant of favour (de Graaf), Adamic administration (Murray), and covenant of love (Stam), among others; as well as terms for the second covenant such as the covenant of reconciliation (Burgess, Ball), covenant of grace (the commonest term), covenant of the gospel (Davenant), or evangelical covenant (Sedgwick). Such terminology can be discussed within the bounds of the TFU, and we should grant each other room for this.

In conclusion, we are in unity with our URC brothers in affirming the uniqueness of Adam's relationship to God pre-fall compared to his and humanity's situation post-fall. In other words, Adam's situation while in a state of righteousness yet able to sin (*posse peccare*) was radically different from our situations in the states of unrighteousness wherein we can only sin (*non posse non peccare*) and of justification by grace through faith wherein we are enabled not to sin (*posse non peccare*).

Key Considerations concerning the Covenant after the Fall, or the Covenant of Grace

Concerning Questions 2 & 3 and Theses on the Covenant of Grace

1. Concerning the relationship between the covenant of grace and election, it is clear that the two are not identical even though they are connected to each other in significant ways. To mention but one obvious difference, election is a decree that God made before the creation of the world (Eph 1:4), while the covenant of grace is a relationship initiated by God after the fall and in history (Gen 15:18). Furthermore, not every child of the covenant is elect (Rom 9:6-13). In this sense, there is a certain duality in the covenant: there were both elect and reprobate among the circumcised in the OT, just as there are both elect and reprobate among the baptized in the NT. Another way of expressing this is that the circle of the covenant is larger than the circle of the elect.

2. The more challenging question is: what is the best way to describe the aforementioned duality in a scripturally responsible and pedagogically effective way? Over time various terms have been proposed: external and internal, administration and essence (substance), or conditional and absolute. Although these terms

attempt to express the truth of the previous point (#1 above), they do have limitations. For example, the following can be mentioned:

    a. although not decisive in and of itself, it is noteworthy that these terms do not appear in Scripture or our confessions;

    b. although the proponents of these terms often wish to prevent it, it does happen that the dual aspect of one covenant becomes, for all intents and purposes, two distinct covenants in the minds of God's people—an external covenant and an internal covenant—while our confessions speaks of one covenant of grace (BC 34; LD 27; CoD 1:17) with two dispensations, old and new (LD 27);

    c. these terms can leave parents in the pew, who are holding their just-baptized baby, in a state of uncertainty, wondering whether their child is *really* in the covenant or not;

    d. these terms do not always do full justice to the scriptural reality of covenant breakers and profaners (Lev 26:15; Deut 31:16,20; Mal 2:10; Heb 10:29): if someone is only externally or conditionally in the covenant can he *truly* break it?

3. Considering the aforementioned limitations, it is helpful to take another look at the terminology that is found in Scripture, namely, that of the blessings (Deut 28; Gal 3:7-14) and the curses (Deut 29:1, 9-14; Gal 3:15-18) of the covenant. These passages shift our attention from *aspects* of the covenant to *outcomes* of life within the covenant. Clearly, there are two different outcomes for covenant people, those who believe "are blessed along with Abraham, the man of faith" (Gal 3:9) and those who do not embrace Christ by faith are under the curse (Gal 3:13-14). In this way, there is a clear confession of one covenant, while the two

outcomes express the duality which was already mentioned in point #1 above.

4. At the same time, there is more than a difference in outcomes (#3 above), there is also a difference in the way that individual believers live *within* the covenant. Someone can merely "go through the motions" and live within the covenant in a merely external and superficial manner. This is ungodly hypocrisy. Conversely, someone can live within the covenant genuinely, that is to say, from the heart in true dedication to, and in fellowship with, the Lord. This is the way it should be. Yet both kinds of people can be found within the covenant, as the apostle Paul indicates in Rom 2:28-29. Here an analogy may help. The Lord compares his covenant with his people to a marriage covenant (Jer 31:32, Eph 5:22-33, etc). Just as a couple can be truly and legally married yet not live together in true harmony and love, so too people may be truly and legally part of the covenant, but not live in genuine faith and love toward the LORD.[5]

5. In addition much can be gained by emphasizing the two parts of the covenant: promise and obligation (Gen 17:4, 9; *Form for Baptism*). If the preacher emphasizes both parts, in the right order and in a balanced way, his congregation will not walk away with the impression that one is automatically saved simply because he is baptized. Furthermore, the obligation is, in the first place, a call to trust the LORD and believe in the covenant

---

5. In its main lines, this is also what L. Berkhof, citing G. Vos, is saying on pp 286-87 of his *Systematic Theology* (Grand Rapids: Eerdmans, 1996). It also coheres well with K. Schilder's emphasis on the legal reality of the covenant, even if the communion within the covenant has not yet flourished due to immaturity (in the case of infants) or is being rejected in unbelief (in the case of hypocrites). See Schilder's *Main Points of the Doctrine of the Covenant*, transl. T. Van Laar (s.l.: s.p., 1992), esp. pp. 3, 11-12.

promises he has given, and then, flowing out of that to also live a life of holiness (LD 23-24, 32-33).

6. The doctrine of election should not overshadow the doctrine of the covenant in such a way that doubt, rather than assurance, is cultivated in the hearts of God's people. Believing parents who bring their covenant child forward to be baptized should be certain that their child belongs truly—not merely possibly or potentially—to the covenant of grace. Along the same lines, the maturing Christian should be fully convinced of the reality of God's promises for him, as well as the reality of his obligations toward God, rather than constantly questioning whether he is elect or not, or whether he is actually in the covenant or not. In this respect, the concluding paragraphs of the Canons of Dort regarding "the consolation of afflicted souls" are very much to the point. We read the Canons of Dort precisely to underline the divine origin, full efficacy, and transforming and preserving power of God's sovereign grace, leading us to assurance rather than doubt.

7. With respect to the role of faith, we need to distinguish carefully between justification and sanctification. With respect to justification, faith relies entirely upon, and accepts, the free gift of Christ's perfect righteousness, satisfaction and holiness. This is what we confess when we say that we are saved only by faith and without any merit of our own (LD 23, 32). With respect to sanctification, faith produces the fruits of good works, as described in the letter of James and summarized in BC 24 ("We believe that this true faith . . . regenerates him and makes him a new man.")

Considerations concerning Question 4 and Theses on the Covenant of Grace

1. BC 29 clearly speaks of hypocrites who are *in* the church but not *of* the church. The CanRCs not only confess this truth

with the mouth but also believe it with the heart (to borrow some language from BC 1). Thus, the issue is not with confessing the truth that there are hypocrites in the church, or in the covenant (see #4 above), but rather how this sad reality is best described in theological terms. Here the CanRCs tend *not* to use the terms invisible and visible church. To begin with, such terminology is found neither in Scripture nor in our confessions. In addition, past experiences, particularly in the Netherlands in the time surrounding the Liberation of 1944, have taught us that speaking of an invisible church *can* lead to a certain pluriform view of the church which, practically speaking, often compromises the truth we confess in BC 28, namely, everyone's duty to join the church, being active members within it and respecting the authority of local office bearers. In short, the CanRCs have no difficulty with using the *in* the church but not *of* the church distinction, but we generally avoid the terms invisible and visible church for the reasons stated above.

2. Concerning the translation of BC 29, we do not think there is any significant issue here. The sentence in question reads: "With respect to those who are members of the Church, they may be known by the marks of Christians; namely, by faith, and when, having received Jesus Christ the only Saviour, they avoid sin, etc" (URCNA Psalter-Hymnal) or "Those who are of the church may be recognized by the marks of Christians. They believe in Jesus Christ the only Saviour, flee from sin, etc."[6] The question revolves around the presence of the word "when" (Fr. *quand*). First of all there is a textual issue that adds a certain wrinkle in the translation history of this sentence. The original text of 1561 did not have *quand ayans recue un seul Sauveur Iesus Christ*, but rather *ce qu'ils reçoyvent un seul Sauveur Iesus Christ*. Now, the *textus receptus* (Synod of Dort 1618-19) certainly does have

---

6. As worded in the CanRC *Book of Praise*.

quand, but the different word choice between the original and the *textus receptus* already indicates something about the semantic force of the word *quand* in that sentence. In that case the word is not suggesting that church members must at a certain point in time receive the Lord Jesus Christ in some kind of special conversion experience. Rather, it is logically connecting the various marks, or indications, that ought to be noticeable in the life of a sincere Christian, specifying that the works of sanctification are not simply parallel with the gift of faith, but flow from it. We fully agree with this, as is clear from many other places in the confessions. Whether the word *quand* is there (as in the *textus receptus* & URCNA Psalter Hymnal) or not there (as in 1561 edition & CanRC translation), the meaning of the sentence remains the same. As a matter of interest, an earlier translation of the BC used in CanRC had the word "when" in it (see *Book of Praise* 1972). The word "when" was removed in a linguistic and stylistic revision in the early 1980s. We have consulted some internal archive documents of that revision process, and we have the distinct impression that the change was made simply for linguistic reasons (i.e., ease of English expression) and not theological reasons.

3

Colloquium at Synod Visalia, June 4, 2014

BOUWERS, GODFREY, VAN RAALTE, VAN VLIET, VENEMA

Moderator, Rev. Bouwers:
I invite our brothers to come and join me here. A hearty welcome to the brothers Dr. Cornel Venema and Dr. Robert Godfrey of the United Reformed Churches, as they come to join me here. We will see which side they sit on, on the right or on the left? And the brothers Dr. Jason Van Vliet and Dr. Ted Van Raalte of the Canadian Reformed Theological Seminary in Hamilton as they join me as well.

I trust you brothers from Hamilton have been made to feel at home with the singing of Psalm 47 as we have it now from out of your *Book of Praise*, a wonderful Genevan. I hope you were encouraged by that.

So, we will not take more of the brothers' time. We've been allotted by synod a generous amount of time for this discussion. We are going to give the brothers an hour amongst themselves.

Following which we are going to have opportunity to interact with them and raise questions or concerns that we might have.

Not much more needs to be said by way of introduction, I trust, in terms of your having received and read the material as synodical delegates. The brothers are first going to give a brief summary of the material. Then they are going to begin the dialogue with one another in this colloquy, or colloquium.

We pray for the Lord's rich blessing on all of the preparations that have been made. We are very grateful for you men, for your willingness to serve the churches in this way. We are grateful for the labors you have put into this and for your willingness to travel all the way here to be with us. We pray and trust that it will be of blessing for us in seeking to understand one another better, and bringing us to clarity, Lord willing, in terms of the matters that are before us.

The particular question that we have before us is the matter of where we find ourselves within the Confessions. And if there are concerns that we have over against one another with regard to our respective "covenant views," the question needs to be asked: Does this, or does this not fit within our confessional commitments together? That needs to be our governing focus in all that we do here tonight.

One of the things that we have experienced as the CERCU committee in various settings throughout various opportunities, is the blessing that the Apostle John speaks about, both in the ending of 2nd John and of 3rd John: "I would have written you, but I wanted to see you face to face." So here, we have received the writings in preparation for the colloquium, and now we have the opportunity in this large setting to see one another face to face, to sit across from one another, to speak with one another and to dialogue with one another in everybody's hearing. And, we trust that will be of mutual benefit, that the Lord will bring us to greater clarity in all of these matters that are before us.

So, once again, a hearty thank-you for your willingness to join us, and the Lord's richest blessing in what we do together!

In terms of the format for the evening, the first hour will be devoted to the brothers speaking among themselves. The first fifteen minutes, seven and half minutes per federational representation, will be for introducing the matter. This will be followed by about thirty to thirty five minutes for dialoging amongst yourselves. And then five minutes each for some closing statements. At that point we will open the floor for questions, concerns, and clarifications. Those questions will be limited to the delegates of synod as this is a synodical colloquy.

We are going to ask the brothers from the United Reformed Churches' side to begin.

Dr. Cornel Venema:

Thank you Rev. Bouwers. Let me begin by expressing my gratitude for the opportunity to participate in this colloquium. I know the time of synod is precious, so giving up a couple of hours on this evening is quite a gift. I hope we use the time wisely in a way that is helpful to the synod and to our federations as we discuss the question of unity and what needs to be done in order to achieve that unity.

Now, Dr. Godfrey has for some reason allowed me to take up all of our seven and a half minutes. It may be his desire to reserve the right not to be responsible for whatever I have to say. So, I am not assuming this seven and a half minute time-slot; it was granted to me by Dr. Godfrey and that's why only one of us is speaking at the outset here, whereas two of the brothers from the Canadian Reformed Churches will be making their opening statement.

Now, to the statement. I'd like to underscore my understanding of what this colloquy aims to achieve. And that is that we keep the focus on the question: Are there between our federations, in terms of our understanding of the doctrine of the covenants, or the covenant, differences of formulation, emphasis, or teaching, that would prevent *unity*, because they in some sense are judged to be in conflict, or outside of the boundaries of what we confess is taught in the Word of God in the Three Forms of Unity? It is very important that we keep that focus clearly before us. What we are asking is, as we discuss together our understanding of the covenant: is that understanding, with whatever particular emphasis or formulation that may be prevalent or present in one or another of our federations, a formulation that we recognize to be within the boundaries of what we believe the Scriptures to teach as confessed in the Confessions.

> Are there between our federations, in terms of our understanding of the doctrine of the covenants, or the covenant, differences of formulation, or emphasis, teaching, that would prevent *unity*

I think it is important for us to remember (just a comment in that connection), that in the history of the Reformed Churches (at least in the Continental Reformed church tradition) probably no topic has been more often the occasion of disagreement, of even separation and schism in the churches, than the topic that is before us. It is a very sensitive topic. It needs to be handled carefully. We need to avoid the temptation to represent the other's position in the worst possible light, or to find reason to be in disagreement where no such reason really exists.

At the same time we have to seek clarity and be frank and direct with each other, to make sure that we are secure in the conviction that there are no differences of a Confessional nature between us.

I say all of this simply to underscore the difficulty of the task. We haven't done well in the history of the Reformed Churches at addressing this question without separating and going our distinct ways.

Now, I assume that all of the delegates received from CERCU the materials, the summary of the exchange that took place between Dr. Van Raalte and Dr. Van Vliet with Dr. Godfrey and myself. So I am not going to attempt to review with you all of that material. I assume that you have it. I just want to say a few things about why we presented the summary in the form in which we did.

Now again I make a disclaimer, and it is this: we do not presume, as we indicated in our introduction, to suggest that what we are summarizing is the view held by all office-bearers in the United Reformed Churches, or that there isn't a very significant range of opinion. There might be members of the United Reformed Churches who think that the brothers from the Canadian Reformed Churches express better their view than we have expressed it. But we are trying to, as best as we can, call attention to our understanding of what we judge to be a very common view of the covenant in the United Reformed Churches. And doing so in a way that is perhaps a bit provocative. That is, calling attention, even deliberately, to where there may be differences of emphasis or accents, so that we have an honest exchange between us.

Now you might ask, why did we start with the doctrine of the covenant of works—the pre-fall covenant relationship that God-Triune establishes as Creator of the human race in Adam, when in the Three Forms of Unity the language of "covenant of works" is not explicitly employed? Well, we did that for two reasons. One, we recognize that it's not language that is always favored in the Canadian Reformed Church tradition. But also because we do believe that the rudiments, or the main elements of the doctrine of what historically has been called a covenant of works are present, not only in the Scriptures, but echoed also in our

Confessions, the Three Forms of Unity. And this is a doctrine commonly affirmed among us as in keeping with Scriptures and our Confessions.

It's a significantly important doctrine because it relates to a doctrine often in discussion, the doctrine of justification. [The question is:] was the work of Christ, as Mediator of the covenant of grace . . . [was it] the work in which all of our obligations under the law of God—first set forth in the covenant of works—were met on our behalf by him? [Were these obligations met] through his active obedience, or perfect obedience to that law, as well as by his substitutionary endurance of the sanction? [The sanction] that [I mean] is, "on the day that you eat thereof, you will surely die" [Gen 2:17], that is, the day that Adam, representing us, would offend against God's holy law, he would come under the curse and come under judgment? [That now is] the curse and judgment in which all of us who are conceived and born in sin, are born.

We attempted to set forth there as best we could what we would regard as a consensus understanding of the doctrine of that covenant. God entered into a relation with the human race, a covenantal relationship in Adam. [It was] a relationship in which Adam was required and obliged to obey God's holy law, to meet the standard of what's often called the probationary command. And that Adam's failure to do so plunged the whole race into sin, and is the occasion, at least in terms of history, for the provision of another covenant, the covenant of grace, whose Mediator is the greater-than-Adam, the last Adam, the Lord Jesus Christ who has done for us under the law, both in terms of its obligations and its sanctions everything needed in order to restore us, if we participate in his righteousness by faith, to favor and right-standing with God.

I won't say anything more about our summary of the doctrine of the covenant of works.

In terms of the doctrine of the covenant of grace . . .

Moderator:
There is just less than one minute.

Dr. Venema:
Less than one minute on the covenant of grace!

Let me say this. The summary that we provide there, if you've read our report, I trust you have, begins with several points where I think there really is no historically significant dispute, debate, or difference of formulation between our respective federations.

I think where we in the latter part of that section want to call to your attention what has often been a point in dispute between our respective traditions is the extent to which we should relate the doctrine of the covenant to the biblical doctrine that we confess in the *Canons of Dort*, the doctrine of election. And we argue there that it is important, in terms of the doctrine of the covenant, to remember that the covenant of grace is a covenant consisting of *promises* of salvation and life through Jesus Christ and faith in him that *obliges* those to whom that promise is addressed—believers and their children—to respond in the way of faith and repentance. It's *outcome* if one does believe is saving blessing and life and communion with God, or, if one does not believe, further condemnation and judgment. In those respects there seems to us to be very little reason for disagreement or difference of emphasis between us. What we emphasize there ([an aside] and I am summarizing, Rev. Bouwers!) is that if you read the language of the *Canons of Dort*, particularly Head of Doctrine II, the Rejection of Errors, you will find that the authors of the *Canons* are concerned to emphasize that God does more in the covenant of grace than simply make promises with appropriate accompanying demands. Ultimately, he by the work of the Mediator of the covenant of grace both procures the blessings of redemption and applies them unfailingly to all those whom he has purposed to elect unto salvation in Christ Jesus.

Therefore, some distinction is needed in our understanding of the covenant of grace between the covenant in its broader administration to believers and their seed, and the covenant in terms of its saving efficacy in the instance of those to whom God gives, according to his purpose of election, what he requires of them, in that covenant relationship.

Moderator:
Thank you. And on that happy note. That's an encouragement!

Dr. Robert W. Godfrey:
[Humorously interjects] I will concede the rest of our time.

Moderator:
Thank you. And with no corrections!
   Dr. Van Raalte will now speak first.

Dr. Ted Van Raalte:
Thank you very much. Thank you for the invitation. It is a trust committed to us to represent the Canadian Reformed Churches to all of you. It is a joy to do so, and a daunting task. But you should also understand that in the end we are representing our own views. We are certainly within the pale of the Canadian Reformed Churches, but we can't speak for everyone and say everyone holds to the same thing. There is a variety among us, also.

   I thought for my opening statement, that I would explain some of the Latin that was in the covenant of works part of our submission. I was largely responsible for that part. We talk about the four-fold state of man. Man being created *posse peccare*, which just means "able to sin." And then once sinning, man is "not able not to sin," *[non posse non peccare]* but in redemption we are "en-abled not to sin," *[posse non peccare]* and in consummation, when Christ returns, we are "no longer able to sin" *[non posse peccare]*. That's a nice little survey of all of redemptive history.

The first state of man, "able to sin," we relate to Genesis 2:17: "but you must not eat from the tree of the knowledge of good and evil for when you eat of it you will surely die." Now, sometimes my Catechism students wondered about that. How could Adam and Eve even know what death was; there was no death before the fall. But Adam and Eve had to understand the language God used, so intellectually they knew that death was possible though they had not yet experienced death themselves. When God says, on the day you eat of it you shall surely die, he teaches them that they have a possible instability. That's the flip side of the freedom-of-choice which he had awarded to them so that their love for him would be genuine, heartfelt and of the creature. And we exercised that liberty against the Lord, and found out what the result was: freedom-of-choice was against God. So it's not a *potential* instability, it's not a potency that just has to come to act, but it is a *possible* instability based on the freedom-of-choice. What that entails, or what that teaches Adam and Eve is: find your stability in the Lord, find your strength in the Lord. Make him your foundation, even in this pre-fall situation.

But then, having fallen into sin, we come to the state of "not able not to sin." Those controlled by the sinful nature *cannot* please God, Romans 8:8. The sinful mind is hostile to God, Romans 8:7. But then, the state of redemption, which describes us in the present era: "You, however are controlled not by the sinful nature but by the Spirit, if the Spirit of God lives in you." Here is our state of "able not to sin." And then our final state of "not able to sin" we can infer from at least two places in Scripture: the one being First Corinthians 15, that the resurrection body will be imperishable, it will be immortal, in order that we may inherit eternal life; the other, Revelation chapter 21, there is no longer any death, there is no longer any curse, sin is taken away, and in the new creation we can dwell with God, forever.

How am I doing for time? Done? Okay, thank you!

Dr. Jason Van Vliet:

I would also like to begin by saying thank you for the invitation here. And I would like to ensure our Moderator for this evening, that we have felt very welcome, and that did not begin when we sang the first Genevan tune, but long, long before that. So, thank you very much.

Genesis 15:17. I would like to read a couple of verses with you: "When the sun had gone down and it was dark, behold, a smoking fire pot and a flaming torch passed between these pieces [pieces of the animals that Abram had put there at the Lord's command]. On that day the LORD made a covenant with Abram, saying, 'To your offspring I give this land, from the river of Egypt to the great river, the river Euphrates, the land of the Kenites, the Kenizzites, the Kadmonites, the Hittites, the Perizzites, the Rephaim, the Amorites, the Canaanites, the Girgashites and the Jebusites.'"

On that day the Lord made, literally *cut*, a covenant with Abraham. On this day, or this evening, we are not going to cut covenant, but in a manner of speaking we may be dissecting the doctrine of the covenant. I think it's helpful from the start, brothers, and sisters here as well, that we keep the connection between that day in which the Lord cut a covenant with our forefather Abram, and this day when we are discussing various details of the doctrine of the covenant. I don't know what's all going to come up—there may be questions about conditions in the covenant, merit in the pre-fall covenant, the matter that has already been brought up, the connection between covenant and election—all of these things. But when we are finished speaking this evening, I would hope that also through the discussions, we have a deep sense of awe! Because that's what Abram had on that day. I didn't read all those verses for the sake of the time, but it's clear from verse 12 that Abram was in a very deep, and even, as Scripture says a dreadful darkness, there was a deep sense of awe. The LORD Almighty has cut covenant! With him, a small, mortal human being! And the LORD Almighty has cut covenant with him and given him these great promises. He, at that point, wasn't looking for covenant. He was looking for a son. He wanted a baby boy to hold in his arms. The LORD cut covenant with him.

That covenant—a couple of chapters later will reveal this in more detail—is the everlasting covenant, which only increases the awe. The LORD Almighty has cut *everlasting* covenant with us? And not only with us, but as it says in chapter 17, with our descendants after us? What wonder of grace! What manner of kindness, undeserved glory, is this? And I hope that in all the details, we don't lose sight, brothers and sisters, of just what an awe-inspiring doctrine this ought to be.

Do I have a little more time?

Moderator:
30 seconds.

Dr. Van Vliet:
Ah, that's great because all I have to do in 30 seconds is introduce covenant and election, and that's no problem [facetiously said]! What I would like to say on that topic, as I am sure we are going to get into this evening, is that, obviously from the history that Dr. Venema has described, it's a very challenging thing. And I don't think that on this evening in two hours we are going to nail down the definitive approach. That would be rather presumptuous on our part. Nevertheless, it seems to me, and maybe this will get us going in our discussion, that the challenge is on the one hand, to not let those two doctrines drift too far apart, but on the other

hand, to not overlap them to the point that they become equated as one and the same thing. The challenge is to chart between those two.

Moderator:
Okay, thank you very much! All of you, Dr. Godfrey included, for all of your contributions. So, at this point we are opening it up for mutual interaction and whoever would like to go first, may.

Dr. Godfrey:
Well, since I've been so well-behaved to this point, let me first of all say that I've always had a very high opinion of Rev. John Bouwers, until he invited me to be a part of this enterprise. And it seemed to me from the outset that I was not a good choice because developments in the Netherlands from the 1940s on is not my area of expertise. And so I need publically to say that almost all of the work on our side has been done by Cornel Venema and I am very grateful to Cornel for his wisdom and involvement from the United Reformed side. The only substantial contribution I made to our statement was the marvelous quotation from Turretin, which is worth the price of all that paper.

I want to say at the outset that I don't know exactly what we are supposed to do now (there may be a question coming at some point). As I tried to get involved in this process I've found it a very helpful learning experience. I sat back and I said, since I don't know in detail much about the controversy in the Netherlands and the extent to which the separation of 1944 was carried over into Canada by the Canadian Reformed, what I do know is what I've heard over the years as a measure of criticism of what we might call Schilderite theology. I don't know if you appreciate that label or not, but . . . alright, *Vrijgemaakt* (Liberated) theology.

And, what I have heard as criticism was, as I thought about it, reducible to three points, relative to covenant.

The first was that Liberated theology was *too objective* and therefore did not have adequate place for the *subjective* doctrine of regeneration in Reformed theology.

Secondly, that it was too *communal* and therefore did not have an adequate place for the *individual* response of faith, which perhaps we could relate to the doctrine of justification.

And, thirdly, that its theology was too *exclusive*, claiming, some contended, that only they were the true church.

So, I went into the discussions we have had with the brothers here with those questions in the back of my mind: What do they really make of covenant and regeneration, covenant and justification, and covenant and true church. And what I discovered was something a historian should never have to discover, namely that we have very different histories. And, as a result of those different histories, we do tend to talk a slightly different language. As I've enjoyed our conversations, what dawned on me, really only yesterday, is that the Dutch Reformed experience in the United States has been heavily shaped and colored and directed by the far larger dominance of Reformed theology in the United States, represented by Presbyterianism. Relative to the size of the Presbyterian churches in America in the 19th and 20th century, the Dutch Reformed churches have been much smaller. Many Dutch Reformed leaders have been educated in Presbyterian institutions, and, as a result, our thinking in Dutch Reformed churches in the United States has been significantly coloured by the Westminster Standards, since that's what coloured Presbyterian thinking.

Now that that's not as terrible as some people might think, because I think that in the 17th and 18th century, most Reformed Christians, whether Scottish, or Dutch, or Swiss, or Hungarian, were all influenced by the developing Reformed theology that is basically summarized in the Westminster Standards. But I think in the 19th and 20th century, several things happened that led Dutch Reformed churches, and to some extent Presbyterian churches, away from that theological world of the 17th century. And, particularly in the 19th and early 20th century, a lot of reaction and criticism to scholasticism as a very bad thing, led, to much vaguer theological formulations, or at least a less common theological vocabulary. So, at least for me, it was a learning experience to realize that the Canadian Reformed brethren have been far less *Presbyterian-ized*, far less *Westminster-ized*, for better or for worse, and remind us, who sort of take for granted certain kinds of covenant language that is really a 17th century development, that that covenantal language is not actually to be found in the Three Forms of Unity.

I think the work that Cornel did does show that in point of fact that substantial elements of the covenant of works are to be found in the Three Forms of Unity, but that term is not to be found there. We need to recognize that we are coming from a somewhat different cultural-historical-theological world, not worlds in conflict, so much, as worlds that have developed different language because of different circumstances. While in the nature of the case, because of the separation of 1944, our Canadian Reformed brothers have remained very focused on this issue of covenant and what it reveals about the doctrine of baptism, I think that at least for a number of us, at least in the United Reformed Church in the United States, our concerns about covenant have been more focused in our reaction to Barthianism and its conflation of the covenant of works and the covenant of grace, and also in the battle to maintain the Protestant doctrine of justification, which has come under attack in Lutheran circles, in Evangelical circles, and in some Reformed circles in our time. And it's been the passion of some of us to maintain Reformed orthodoxy on those points.

As I have gone through this experience, and this conversation, I have come out feeling very gratified to discover that although we may use slightly different language, I am convinced that at least these two brothers are exactly committed to the doctrine of justification as we are, and that they are committed to the doctrines of regeneration, and similar ecclesiologies to us as well.

I fear that that may disappoint some of you. Perhaps some of you came tonight hoping that we would have "fun" as they did at the great Synod of Dort when Franciscus Gomarus challenged Martinius to a duel on the floor of synod. Being a coward myself, I am willing to let Cornel do that, but presumably it is not necessary.

The question—to which I finally come—was actually about the last page [pp. 21–3 of this book] of the Canadian Reformed response, where they expressed concern about a certain view of the pluriformity of the church. And that was really the only formulation that concerned me, primarily because I am not sure what they mean by that. And it does perhaps relate to this question of true church and what we mean by true church and who is able to qualify to be labeled a true church. So, if I am allowed to ask a question after a long introduction, it would be: could you provide greater clarity for what you see as a danger of a certain pluriform view of the church?

Dr. Van Vliet:

Thank you brother. In some of our discussions leading up to the public discussion, Dr. Godfrey would make comical little remarks about the long-windedness of Dr. Venema. I am not sure that Dr. Venema is the only one who has that distinction . . .

Let me try to address a few things mentioned.

First of all, the difference in background and what was said by Dr. Godfrey, that the United Reformed Churches, because of their history may be more, did you say *Presbyterian-ized*? There's something, brothers, very real about that. The Canadian Reformed Churches, as you understand by the first word in the name of our federation, are predominantly in Canada. We have a few in the United States of America, but very few. And in Canada, there are not a whole lot of really strong, vibrant, confessional Presbyterian churches. The Presbyterian Church of Canada is completely liberal. Once in a while you will find an OPC here or there, or an RPCNA. But it's vastly different than your experience here in the United States of America. You are constantly bumping into OPs and RPCNAs and PCAs. So we've gone through a different history, and are still going through different circumstances which lead to familiarity with certain language, terms, ways of thinking. We need to keep that in mind.

Maybe I can say something about the objective-subjective thing that you mentioned. This ties in with the whole matter of the history. The Canadian Reformed Churches, as a federation, find their birth point in 1944, the Liberation, as you've seen in the document. And, at that time, the teachings of Abraham Kuyper had led to an experience among the people in the pew, concerning baptism, that was very troubling to them. To make a long story short, Abraham Kuyper's understanding of *presumptive regeneration*—you have to presume that there is a seed of regeneration in your child, [and that] the baptism water points to, [or] is a sign of, the seed of regeneration. But what it all ended up in, was that the parents bringing their newborn to the front of the church were uncertain: now, did my child receive real, genuine baptism, or was it something that was kind of just an appearance but didn't connect to reality? In that situation, there was an emphasis on the objective nature of the covenant. When the Lord makes promises, he means it. It's real. You can count on that as parents. When the Lord also gives a sign of the covenant, which includes obligations, that's real.

Now, whenever there is crisis in the church, leading perhaps sadly to a split in the church, we know that certain points become very strong and then we tend to swing the pendulum in the other direction out of that concern. Now, 70 years have gone past since 1944. We've learned that we have to be careful about that. And there is that element of appealing to God's people that's very important, calling them to faith, calling them to repentance, speaking to them in a personal [way], or in a way that has a certain subjective emphasis. So, we all went through histories, and under the Lord's blessing some of these things balance out, over time.

Lest Dr. Godfrey accuse me of being long-winded, I will quickly turn it over to my colleague, Dr. Van Raalte.

Dr. Van Raalte:

Okay, maybe I'll just remark on the "Schilderite" term; I shook my head when you said that. Through four years of Seminary—for me that was '95 through '99—I would really have to search to see if I was ever assigned a reading from Schilder. Schilder is very difficult to translate, you can't expect students to read him in Dutch, and it's hard to find somebody who's willing to actually translate his material. He had a very intricate use of the Dutch language. And we tend to shy away from identifying ourselves with certain people. So for instance, don't call me a Calvinist, I am Reformed. In the same sense, I wouldn't want to say Schilder was the founder of our church. So you mustn't think that the Canadian Reformed Churches are just running on the theology of Klaas Schilder, and I am sure he wouldn't want us to say that either.

We've used Louis Berkhof, probably for four decades. I know Dr. Van Vliet has tried another Dogmatics textbook, and he's gone back to Louis Berkhof with supplements from Herman Bavinck. And I suggest we would find a lot of common ground in Herman Bavinck and his very clear biblical explanations, his reaching into history, and his own reconstruction of doctrine in continuity with the Scholastic Reformers—the Reformation and those thereafter, the Orthodox. So, we prefer to be identified by the term Reformed and say it is the Confessions of Faith and the Scriptures as interpreted in the Confessions of Faith that are the touchstone for us, and the starting point.

Moderator:
If I may, you did have one question directed to you that I don't believe you've addressed?

Dr. Godfrey:
There can be an excessive brevity.

Dr. Van Vliet:
Yes, the matter of pluriformity.

Just to put some context to that, in our discussion, the question from our URC brothers was, why don't you use the terms *invisible church* and *visible church*, [and] connect that to [a] *dual-aspect* of the covenant, speaking perhaps of *internal* and *external* aspects of the covenant . . . why don't you use that language more? Why are you perhaps a little bit reluctant on that? It was that question that we wrote [about] on the last page there, page 15, point 1 [p. 18 in this book]. To say that, particularly in connection with speaking of the *invisible church*. Now as Abraham Kuyper worked with that, and as those who were following Kuyper worked with that, the idea developed that the church in its *real* essence, in what was *really* important, was invisible. Of course, what's invisible is kind of nebulous. But that *invisible church* is manifest in various different forms, therefore: *pluriformity*. So it is manifest in all kinds of different churches here on earth. And, in practical experience, what that led to was people who had a weak consciousness of what it means to find a faithful church of the Lord Jesus Christ, to be involved in that, and to be committed to that, to be under the supervision and discipline of the office-bearers in that faithful church. So it became a very loose commitment to church membership. And because of that experience, connected to that term *invisible*, we've been reluctant to use that word.

What we tried to indicate in what we wrote is that [this is] the heart of the matter: the church of the Lord Jesus Christ, as it's gathered here and as we experience it from Sunday to Sunday under the preaching and administration of the sacraments, *does* contain hypocrites. We confess that in *Belgic Confession* 29. We clearly speak of those who are *in* the church, not just in the church building, they are in the church, they are members of the church, but they are not really *of* the church, because they are putting on a show. They are hypocrites. And whereas some might use the terms *invisible* and *visible church* to get at that reality, and deal with the reality that there are hypocrites in the church, we would tend to use language such as is found in the *Belgic Confession* 29, and speak of those *in* the church, but not *of* the church.

Properly understood, the way the *Westminster Standards* use *invisible* and *visible church*, that's not the same way that Abraham Kuyper was developing it, there's a difference there. And we need to distinguish that.

Dr. Venema:

Since our conversation has been *so* friendly, let me introduce, at least, a question that might be more provocative. We have talked about this, so it doesn't come as a surprise.

I will raise the specter of what is known to many of us as the Federal Vision. I do that not to introduce a red herring into our discussion, but because among those who have advocated what is today referred to as the Federal Vision, some of the principal proponents have cited the influence and persuasiveness of what they understand to be Schilder's doctrine of the covenant, to their own development of the doctrine of the covenant. In doing that, their view involves a couple of things, one in terms of the doctrine of justification within the Federal Vision. The question whether the righteousness that is granted and imputed to us—Christ's obedience under the law in its full respect, *active* and *passive*—is an entire righteousness, necessary to our right-standing with God? Or is it simply his passive obedience that constitutes the righteousness granted and imputed to us? And that argument is often associated with a rejection of the doctrine of the covenant of works. That's why in our presentation, we didn't introduce the doctrine of the covenant of works to introduce a sort of alien Presbyterian notion into the picture. But to call attention to what we understand to be one of its implications, to use a perhaps weak word, namely, that the work of the Mediator, our Lord Jesus Christ, that is necessary for our justification requires that his obedience unto the law be entire. That includes what is sometimes distinguished as his *active obedience*—doing what the law obliges us to do, but doing it in our stead.

I think it would be helpful to the body if you would express how you view that question. I think it is very clear in the materials that were presented. But it will be helpful because the association of a rejection of the doctrine of the covenant of works with a like rejection of the full righteousness of the Lord Jesus Christ, all his merits, as basis for our justification is a question, I think, that is lively among the United Reformed Churches.

While I am on the whole question of the Federal Vision, it is characteristic of the argument of many in the Federal Vision movement, that we really need to hold election and covenant so closely together, that all those to whom the promise of the covenant is addressed, and who receive the sign and seal of the covenant in baptism, and the promise of the covenant, are to be, not simply *regarded* but are actually and in truth, elect persons, having all the saving blessings that are theirs in Christ Jesus, unless and until they should break covenant. So, election, in this formulation, tends to be viewed as temporary and losable, and therefore in a profound sense, conditional. I think it would be helpful to the body—I am not suggesting for a moment that these are your views—but how would you distinguish the doctrine of justification that lives within the Canadian Reformed Churches, and even the doctrine of the covenant, from some of the views, that at least within our federation have been found deeply troubling, in terms of the Federal Vision, in terms of our own actions in that respect?

Dr. Van Raalte:

Okay, that sounds like we have quite a few topics to cover. But where shall we start?

Let's begin with the question of the imputation of the active obedience of Christ. We have taken the position that this is a Confessional matter. It is not up for grabs. Just to read a short portion of page 11 here, 3a [pp. 27–28 in this book]: "Although the debate generated by Piscator"—Piscator here is the first to *deny* the imputation of the active obedience of Christ, saying that Christ was actively obedient, but that this was simply to make him fit for his own office of Mediator; it wasn't to be accounted to us. And so although that debate about the active obedience of Christ, "was subsequent to the composition of the *Belgic Confession* and the *Heidelberg Catechism*"—the debate doesn't start until the 1580s or so and the *Belgic Confession* and the *Catechism* were written in 1561 and 1563—"we affirm that these [confessions of faith] should be understood to affirm the doctrine, on the grounds that the *textus receptus* of the BC, as improved by the Synod of Dort 1618-1619, clearly affirms the doctrine in Article 22, 'he imputes to us all his merits and as many holy works as he has done for us and in our place.'" We note also the closing of HC 23.60, 'He grants these (the righteousness, satisfaction, and holiness of Christ) to me . . . as if I myself had accomplished all the obedience which Christ has rendered for me.' Our *Form for Lord's Supper* celebration also includes, 'By his perfect obedience he has for us fulfilled all the righteousness of God's law.'"

So, (in answer to the question) how do we separate our view from some of the things that have happened in Federal Vision? Well, simply by articulating what we ourselves teach, what we would train our seminary students to follow, and what we think our *Confessions of Faith* teach. Federal Vision can run the whole gamut from being more objective about the covenant promises of God, and we could find some benefit from some of the things they may have written, but then they go on to confuse terms like election, and speak of a temporary justification or a losing of election. That just goes up against the language of the *Canons of Dort* and confuses the people of God. That's not the way we normally talk. Even if you are redefining the term election for yourself in some covenantal way, it's just not helpful. And then, furthermore, Federal Vision can run the gamut all the way to a kind of tri-theism where the unity of the persons of God is not a unity of essence but is a unity of covenant. I would think that we would all repudiate that very quickly.

So, how would we distance ourselves from that? Well, by affirming these things such as we are now and assuring you that certainly these sorts of things don't live among us. There may be a person here or there in the Canadian Reformed circles who says: I've learned a lot from Federal Vision, or, I like that. And I actually wonder then, if they've really immersed themselves in all of the various things that are said? Baptismal regeneration? I mean, since when did baptism do more than the gospel does? So I would just plead that we will try to represent a very biblical approach.

The last thing I would just mention has to do with justification, sanctification, the role of faith, the question of whether faith is to be a living faith when it is the instrument of justification? Of course faith is supposed to be a living faith, but when we are speaking of the matter of justification, we agree with you that law and gospel are antithetical and we mustn't introduce into the receptor of grace, some kind of works. It would adulterate the grace that's given to say that the receptor itself [true faith] is required to be living, obedient, etc. So with respect to justification, faith is an instrument which relies on, trusts in, accepts the promises of the gospel. With respect to sanctification, faith is probably more the efficient cause of good works. But we are going to distinguish those things very carefully.

I can think of Dr. Van Vliet's inaugural address for the Seminary where he mentioned something along the lines that he wasn't going to teach a blender-ized mix of justification and sanctification.

Dr. Van Vliet:

Yep, I said that. You see, a blender is excellent for smoothies. And I enjoy it at home when my wife makes a good smoothie for me. She puts various things in there and my favorite is banana and mango. And you turn it on and the content is great. But you don't do that in Dogmatics! You don't take justification, drop it in there, sanctification, drop it in there, turn it on and blender-ize them all. That's not only going to cause confusion, that's going to compromise the gospel.

Now I hope that we've made it abundantly clear in this document, that when it comes to the *heart* of the gospel, concerning justification, we clearly, and wholeheartedly, and certainly affirm that justification is a) only on the basis of Christ's merit, both in his death, paying the penalty, and in his obedience in our place. And I know that Dr. Van Raalte read it, but I would just like to bring this a little closer to home in that last sentence in 3a (page 11) [p. 28 in this book]. Please remember, brothers, that *every* time that the Lord's Supper is celebrated in Canadian Reformed churches, the following words are heard and affirmed: By his perfect obedience, he (that is, Christ) has for us fulfilled *all* (emphasis added) the righteousness of God's law. That's read usually every two months in every Canadian Reformed Church. Now, with that kind of a statement, even if we don't always use the terminology of *active* and *passive obedience*, [we clearly affirm the truth.] And we don't typically use that terminology because that terminology is not in our Confessions, and when we talk in the midst of the churches we, as a rule, use Confessional language. When we teach at the Seminary, we get into *active* and *passive obedience*, but when I am teaching Catechism I may not talk about *active* and *passive obedience* all of the time. But that's the heart of it, there it is. That's the doctrine. And that's being said from Canadian Reformed pulpits every time the Lord's Supper is celebrated.

Now, just back to Schilder, and I'll be very quick on this one. Dr. Van Raalte hardly had the opportunity to read too much Schilder in his Seminary education, and my education was very similar. We were just a couple of years apart, [we didn't read much Schilder] because not much had been translated. Now, I would like, then to ask the question, even if there are writers out there associated with the Federal Vision movement who have footnoted Schilder here or there, how well does *anyone* in North America understand Schilder, unless they are fluent in the Dutch language? And I've even spoken to those who are perfectly fluent in the Dutch language and they say, "I've never read anything more difficult than Schilder." So we need to be very cautious on that. Just because you footnote someone doesn't mean that there's a complete one-for-one identity between theologies. You can footnote all kinds of different people, [but what that actually means is a different question.]

And then, finally on the covenant of works and covenant of

grace in connection with the doctrine of justification. When you speak with Canadian Reformed brothers, when it comes to defending the doctrine of justification against what I've called blender-izing it with sanctification, then those who are more familiar with *Westminster Standards'* language gravitate towards the distinction—covenant of works / covenant of grace—and that's their tool, that's their go-to instrument in order to defend the doctrine of justification in its purity. We would more likely go to the *Heidelberg Catechism* than the covenant of works / covenant of grace distinction. We, in that endeavour to protect the doctrine of justification, would go to Lord's Days 23 and 24, and point out, particularly in Lord's Days 23 and 24 that works are excluded, very strongly. And the topic of good works only comes later. And we [point out that] the *Catechism* did that on purpose. And it's only in Lord's Day 32 that you start to hear about good works, and then it's framed up as: Christ's second blessing to us of renewing us in his image.

So that's the tool that we would use. We would say, look, don't mix up Lord's Day 23 and 24 with Lord's Day 32. But we are getting at the same thing. We want to defend the same doctrine, but with slightly different tools.

Dr. Venema:

If I may, I appreciate very much what has been said. I suppose I have just one observation: I think it's true that we would more likely go, for example, to the distinction between the covenant of works and the covenant of grace to get a broader, biblical-theological background for insisting that the work of the greater, last Adam is a work that redresses in every respect the consequences of human sin, the failure of Adam under the first covenant. I don't mean to delay the Q and A, but I would be a little bit interested to ask: if you go to the *Catechism* for a warrant for saying that our justification requires the fullness of Christ's righteousness, that of course still leaves the question unanswered, where in the Scriptures is the biblical-theological warrant for the *Catechism's* saying that found? Historically, certainly a very significant, if not an integral component of that Reformed theology has been an understanding of what Adam failed to do and lost by his sin and disobedience, and what our Lord Jesus Christ, in his place, for our salvation, has accomplished for us in doing what Adam did not do and suffering the consequence that results from Adam's failure on our behalf. It would seem to me that's a pretty big, broad-stroked and rather common basis in the broad tradition of Reformed theology.

Dr. Van Vliet:
And one that resonates completely.

Dr. Van Raalte:
Yeah, I believe that resonates completely. About the Adam-Christ parallel: I've heard it much in our Reformed preaching, I've used it myself. We reflect on these things carefully also, and if I might, I'll just read a short paragraph of something that I myself have written and presented to colleagues. Maybe a few people here have heard it before, but, at the time I read it really fast. Now I will do it slower. I want to do this just to show you that we can reflect on these things as well at a theological level, for the purposes of rightly understanding the work of Christ, and, with power, presenting Christ as our Savior and Mediator.

> First, regarding the passive obedience of Christ, I understand that to mean that he took upon himself the curse of the law incurred by our sins. He bore an infinite wrath which he could do by the power of his infinite divine essence, as we confess in Canons of Dort II, articles 1–4. This suffering and death of Christ pays for all that we have done

wrong and as such returns us to the Garden (He paid the price, we are at least back to Adam in the Garden).

Second, I also think that Christ fulfilled the covenant of works in Adam's place. We may call this his active obedience. I relate this particular to his human nature and term it a finite active obedience. I read Romans 5:18 to describe Adam and Christ as two federal heads, and thus I have no problem calling Christ the Mediator and Head of the elect, as we confess in Canons of Dort I, 7. But what did Christ achieve by the active obedience that fulfilled the requirements of the covenant of works? I suggest he perfectly keeps the law and supplies the perfect, personal, and perpetual obedience God required. This finally passes the test in the Garden of Eden. Christ did not transgress the command not to eat of the tree and he kept all the commands of the moral law. But there is no evidence that this obedience alone is sufficient to bring us to the eschaton (Right? The "not able to sin" condition). For this we turn to the fact that he is Mediator according to both natures (which is always important for the Reformed over against the Lutherans). In his passive obedience the unity of his person ensures that he can bear an infinite wrath in his human nature by the power of his divine nature (Heidelberg Catechism, QA 17). In his active obedience, the unity of his person ensures that his human nature did not falter when an obedience was required of it which no human could endure. He had to set his face to the cross and go there because God had commanded it through prophecy. This was commanded of no one else. He had to do so all the while having the power, with one wish of his heart, to call on ten legions of angels, or, to come down from the cross. It took an infinite power to be obedient to the Father, and I would suggest that this is what takes us finally to the new creation.

Bearing the curse and obeying the same law we had to obey was not enough. He also had to submit to the very role that from eternity he had agreed to take, and this was God's way to the new creation where we would no longer be able to sin, where the possibility of a fall will have been taken away.

Thus far.

Moderator:

Thank you very much.

Brothers from the URC side, could you give us a quick summary before we go to the question period?

Dr. Venema:

We are hesitating because we are not sure who of us can be quickest? Neither.

I don't really have a prepared summary. I think the discussion that we've had thus far confirms what Dr. Godfrey and I have experienced in our discussion with Drs. Van Raalte and Van Vliet. That is, though we have some differences by virtue of history and other kinds of influences, I don't think that we've found in the course of our discussions back and forth that there was a matter of substance that touched upon our integrity in terms of the Confessions. If they are willing to live with our formulation, where it might at certain points have a little different emphasis than their own, and we likewise, theirs, I think that's in the main our general sense of what our discussions together have led us to conclude: that we do not judge that what we've heard from them is something that puts them outside of the boundaries. And I think it's important to use the language of boundaries. The Confessions do not limit every possible difference of emphasis and formulation on these questions that have existed within the Reformed churches for a long time. And there is a freedom that's permissible within those boundaries, that I don't think has been violated.

Dr. Godfrey:

Could I just say very briefly, that for many of us the development in the 17th century of discussions of covenant of works and covenant of grace were precisely an effort to clarify and defend the 16th century distinction between law and gospel. And [we think] that whatever needs to be said to protect the work of Christ and the Reformed doctrine of justification is present in the law/gospel distinction as well as in the covenant of works/ covenant of grace distinction.

Let me say, as one who has been beat about the head any number of times by people who call themselves Reformed, accusing me of being a Lutheran for promoting the law/gospel distinction, that I am particularly gratified to the brothers for writing: "We agree that in the decisive matter of the believer's justification, law and gospel are antithetical concepts." I love you for that.

And let me say that Dr. Van Vliet is to be congratulated for having anyone remember anything he said in his inaugural lecture. My experience is that those things are not usually well remembered, but congratulations again.

Dr. Van Vliet:

You will have to ask him, but it may be the only thing he remembers from that address.

Dr. Van Raalte:
I wasn't even there. [laughter]

Dr. Van Vliet:
So it was just gossip. [laughter]

Summing up, we have the same Word of God. And I realize to say that is, on the one hand, a beautiful privilege, but [on the other hand] it's a little bit too simple. Because there are all kinds of different churches, and people of all kinds of different theologies [who] can say they have the Word of God. But in addition to having the same Word of God, we have exactly the same Confessional Standards, the Three Forms of Unity. And then I realize that even that may be a little too simple because beyond the language that we find in the *Three Forms of Unity*, we have theological dialogue and discussions and we have terms and phrases that we use, and sometimes we sense different nuances. And the one that we've kind of identified here, I think, Dr. Godfrey, from the beginning, is that as Canadian Reformed Churches we haven't gone through the kind of being *Presbyterianized* that, at least some of, you have. But, might I add, brothers, that some time after the *Vrijgemaakt* came to this good Continent, they started to come in contact with the OPC. And we—as the OPC brothers will know—have had very, very extensive discussions, also on these points of visible church and invisible church, covenant of works and covenant of grace, and all these kinds of things. But at the end of the day, after we talked about it long and hard, it was deemed to be, by the Canadian Reformed Churches, *no* obstacle to fellowship. We have a sister church relationship with the OPC, just as you do yourselves. So, that demonstrates that even when more Westminsterian language is used, it may not be what we are accustomed to using historically, but we never regarded that as being an obstacle. It's within the bounds of how we can work.

THE BOND OF THE COVENANT WITHIN THE BOUNDS OF THE CONFESSIONS

L to R: Dr. Van Raalte, Dr. Van Vliet, Rev. Bouwers, Dr. Venema, Dr. Godfrey

4

Question Period at Synod Visalia June 4, 2014

BOUWERS, GODFREY, VAN RAALTE, VAN VLIET, VENEMA

Moderator:
Thank you very much brothers. That's been very helpful and encouraging. So at this point we are going to open the floor to the delegates for questions. So, go ahead.

Rev. Michael Brown:
Well first I just want to thank you, all the brothers, for participating in this, and thank you to the convening consistory and whoever's responsible for putting on this colloquium. This is a great use of our time at Synod and far more enjoyable than many of the things that we do. And thank you (Canadian Reformed) brothers. As an American URC minister, it's great to get to know you, to read what you believe concerning covenant theology, how much overlap we have, and how much we are saying the same things, but maybe using different language. And,

clearly your love for the gospel is evident, so I want to thank you for that.

I just have two questions, for my own sake, to get to know the CanRC better, which is what this colloquium is partly about, both on covenant theology. One, with regard to the covenant of redemption, the *pactum salutis*, you know, the doctrine that there was an inter Trinitarian covenant before the foundation of the world. I think I heard it referenced maybe in that paragraph that [Dr. Van Raalte read]. How widely held is that in the CanRC?

Dr. Van Raalte:
I don't know how widely held it is. We could talk about the use of the *Canons of Dort* in the Canadian Reformed Churches, which I think is quite robust. I myself, on the basis of the many things in Scripture, hold to a form of it: this election is from before the creation of the world, Ephesians 1. How about Isaiah 49 and the Servant of the Lord who is bargaining with the Lord, and the Lord says you have to save my people and gather them from the East and from the West and so on. And then the servant sounds a little bit hesitant and the Lord says, it's not enough for you to do this, you are going to bring in the Gentiles also. And when you think, when does a discussion like that take place, it just pushes you into and towards a *pactum salutis*. Now once again, we are talking, what shall we say, scholastic theology, which for me is good, I like that, though some people don't like the term.

Now, you don't go to your congregation and mention *pactum salutis* in your sermon. However, do you affirm that the Sovereign God, from before the creation of the world chose his own? [Do you affirm] that this love of God arises from his own heart—it's his electing love; that the death of the Lord Jesus Christ is an effective grace that effectively redeemed all those for whom he died; that the work of the Holy Spirit is a transforming grace, changing their hearts; and that the Triune God, Father, Son and Holy Spirit, is preserving his own until the end?

Maybe I should speak just a little bit more about the use of the *Canons of Dort*. When I had my preparatory exam to be eligible for call, Rev. Clarence Stam assigned me the *Canons of Dort*. Okay? You have to know the *Canons of Dort*. So I asked him, which section? *The Canons of Dort,* the whole thing! It was a huge blessing in my life, because it was an opportunity to just pull together all the things that were in there. And I've just been so thankful for that assignment ever since. And we have, from early on already, Dr. Jelle Faber, who was our dogmatician for what was it, thirty years? Twenty at least. He had a book called *The Bride's Treasure* together with several other authors. It was a commentary on the *Canons of Dort*. We have Clarence Bouwman who gave post-confession classes on the Canons of Dort and one of his students dutifully wrote down everything he said. That's what Calvin had, right [i.e., an amanuensis]? Peter Feenstra is another one of our ministers who has a commentary on the *Canons of Dort*. Catechism classes: my students always got the *Canons of Dort* for an entire year. Not all ministers do that the same way. Some stick more tightly to the *Catechism*, but a lot of us make sure our students get the *Catechism, Belgic Confession* and the *Canons of Dort*. And so I would say that it is fairly alive and well. And, I have preached on Rev. Freswick's pulpit on Romans 8. And he let me do it twice, so . . .

Rev. Brown:
So, it's not uncommon to meet CanRC ministers who hold to the covenant of redemption as a doctrine?

Dr. Van Raalte:
I don't know.

Dr. Van Vliet:

The only thing I would add to what my colleague has said already is that certainly whatever is there in the *Canons of Dort*, we affirm wholeheartedly, robustly. Now, the question is then, do you want to take part of what is in the *Canons of Dort* and put the label *pactum salutis* on it, or covenant of redemption? Some CanRC ministers may do that, others wouldn't. But I would just remind all of us here that not even the *Westminster Standards* do that.

So, we tend to be careful about using confessional language, especially in our work in and among the people. And then, when we are sitting here talking as ministers, or in the Seminary classroom, we will talk about other things, but when it comes to God's people, we try to use confessional language as much as possible.

Rev. Brown:

That's helpful, thank you.

My other question was with regard to the Mosaic covenant and its relationship with the one unifying covenant of grace. As you both know, there's been a variety of views and nuances in the 16th and 17th Century about how that relationship works, including the view that somehow the Mosaic covenant republished or re-enacted, as Charles Hodge said, or was a re-statement as John Owen said, of the pre-fall covenant, usually using this for protection of justification, the law/gospel distinction. This was not in any way saying it was for individual salvation, but relating it only to Israel's land promises. So, that doctrine, is that something that you would see outside the bounds of the *Three Forms of Unity*? Within the bounds? Would you accept a minister who held that kind of view in the CanRC?

Dr. Van Vliet:

We've certainly heard these more recent discussions, as the

intensity increases regarding the republication of the covenant of works in the Mosaic era. I wouldn't want to jump to any quick and rash judgments on this because I would really want to know, in the first place, what exactly that teaching is, what motivates it? I haven't spent hours and hours reading this stuff; there are many things to do in life. But from the reading that I have done, and maybe that's my own dullness . . . but, to be perfectly frank, I just don't get it. What actually is the issue? What is it getting at? And so to say, would that be accepted in the CanRC, would it not be accepted, we have to understand what it's all about before we could properly make any judgments.

Dr. Van Raalte:

I could add a little bit to that. I've never heard it said in the Canadian Reformed Churches that the Mosaic covenant is in some sense a republication of the covenant of works. In fact, it would be, I think, universally said that it is an administration of the covenant of grace, because God says, I am Yahweh your God and here's what I did for you, so that's my grace, and here's my expectation of you and how you will live in grace and prosper in the land. This would be your response. I think that the original context of the Sinaitic legislation is the third use of the law. I realize that that's in dispute, when you bring up the question about whether it's in some sense a republication. So, I think it's fair to say the Mosaic covenant would be viewed as an administration of the covenant of grace. We've never actually come across someone who thought otherwise, and like Dr. Van Vliet said, we'd have to study that in more detail. I have looked at some of the Reformed Baptists in the 17th Century and their debates on covenant theology. They had to grapple with the fact that there are covenants in the Bible as well, but they didn't want to make the inference that circumcision carries over to baptism. And one of the ways that they prevented that was by saying that any command to circumcise belonged to a covenant of works, but the promise of eternal life belonged to the covenant of grace. It ended up being an arbitrary stamp on the Bible which took one text and said, that one's law and the covenant of works and it's revoked—so therefore the command to circumcise doesn't carry over in the command to baptize the infants. I am familiar with that, but that's something different than the doctrine of republication.

Moderator:
Okay, thank you.

Dr. Godfrey:
For your comfort, all those who hold to the *Westminster Standards* and are interested in promoting the idea of republication, are also obligated by the *Westminster Standards* to say in the first place that the Mosaic economy is an administration of the covenant of grace. That's the first thing that has to be said. Republication is a secondary development of reflection on the Mosaic covenant.

Moderator:
Brother Slagter –

Rev. Lou Slagter:
Good evening brothers. Again, thank you very much for everything that's been spoken of. I had one question here that's on page 11 and number 4 [p. 28 of this book] where you say: "We agree that in the decisive matter of the believer's justification, law and gospel are antithetical concepts. Indeed, to affirm this is fundamental to our salvation, as the various confessional references in this thesis affirm (see further our comments on the role of faith . . .)"

There you come out with a robust understanding of how we are justified. A huge amen to that! I wanted to just ask one question. Can you speak about what you wrote in the next sentence? You say: Yet we also affirm that in the language of Scripture the gospel is to be "obeyed" and even includes threats. I know you quoted a couple of texts like John 3 and the like, so I recognize the idea. What you are saying is that you have to embrace the gospel, you have to believe in the Lord Jesus Christ. Is there more to that in what you are saying here? How does the gospel even include threats?

Dr. Van Raalte:

Okay, this is my section so I'll begin here. This is in the spirit of Klaas Schilder, and let me just say why. If you say common grace, what does Klaas Schilder say: what about common curse? If you say church militant and church triumphant, he will say, well isn't the triumphant church calling out that God would avenge their blood, these souls under the altar? So aren't they also militant? Something that he liked to do was to "push back" a little bit and say, let's think about this a little more. You've got a nice theological construction, but does it satisfy all of the language of Scripture? And don't lock yourself into the theological construction to such a point that you can't let Scripture speak anymore. And I think that's the spirit in which this is presented for discussion here, that the gospel even includes threats.

Let's see, I've referenced there 2 Thessalonians 1:8. I believe that's the text—"those who do not obey the gospel of our Lord Jesus Christ." Let me see here. Second Thessalonians 1:8, "He will punish those who do not know God and do not obey the gospel of our Lord Jesus." I can't do a complete exegesis of that right here but let me at least suggest that it would seem that that's speaking of those who do not obey the command to believe and repent. So in that sense the gospel commands, and you should obey. For didn't the Apostle say to the very same church, and this is his first letter as far as we know, 1 Thessalonians 2:13: "We also thank God continually because when you received the Word of God which you heard from us you accepted it not as the word of men but as it actually is, the Word of God which is at work in you who believe." Yeah, they accepted it, but I think it would then also have the sense that they obeyed the call to believe and receive this as the Word of God.

I also had referenced Revelation 3 there: if you are lukewarm I will spit you out of my mouth, and so on. How about this: just thinking that believers also have commands to obey, in fact the whole third use of the law *is* that. Aren't they *gospel* commands in Second Corinthians 6:14 to 7:1, [where we read] what do the unbeliever and the believer have in common? It is obviously written to believers. It's not just to convict them of sin, but to guide them in righteous and holy living, and to say, Christ and Belial have no fellowship, you shouldn't be having associations with unbelievers that are compromising your faith.

And then we've referenced the Latin and French texts of the *Canons of Dort* 5.14 where it clearly says that the gospel threatens. We could go on more, but the sense is, one, that the gospel commands us to believe, and two, as a believer, the commands you receive to walk in the way of righteousness are given to you as a believer. That comes out of the gospel as well.

Dr. Van Vliet:

Just very briefly, in addition to that. What my colleague mentioned a little earlier, I believe is a true point: That we want to be careful with our theological constructions, our frameworks, our terminology . . . [we want to be careful with them so] that we don't adhere to them so rigidly that when we read something that sounds a little bit different in Scripture, for instance that the gospel ought to be obeyed, that we have no more room for that language as well. Obviously we have to let our theological constructs be determined by the language of Scripture. So we have to be careful.

Moderator:
Okay. Brother Postma –

Elder Will Postma:
I too want to thank you all for coming. I am an elder in the United Reformed Churches, and to be honest with you, I maybe speak for many here, the hour was quite short. I would have liked to have heard a little bit more, and not to pick out differences, but actually to enjoy the similarities that exist. And I am very encouraged that I can go back to Kansas City where I am from and make a very positive report of what we've heard here tonight.

We've heard a little bit about some of the doctrinal issues or things that we are connected to one another with. Perhaps from a practical standpoint I have some questions and let's perhaps look at one subject matter in particular, and that's the Lord's Supper. When it comes to the Lord's Supper, we have in our churches, churches that practice differently. Some have weekly communion, some have quarterly, some have monthly. How do the Canadian Reformed Churches practice that? And how do you view our divergent practices?

And then, number 2, we also have what we would call supervised practice. It's my understanding that in the past, the Canadian Reformed Churches have had more of a fencing type practice. Has that changed? How does that work together with our churches today?

Dr. Van Vliet:
Okay, first of all, the first question is simply about the frequency of the Lord's Supper? The most common now in the federation is

six times per year, once every other month. There are churches that do it quarterly. There has also been a church that did it weekly, a small congregation. So there has been variety on the frequency, and I don't see it as being an obstacle.

Then about the supervision of the Lord's Supper. There are certain differences in the way that we handle the matter of the supervision of the Lord's Supper. We are most familiar with an attestation system, which may be unfamiliar to at least some of you. With an attestation, the home consistory gives testimony that [a certain] brother, or brother and sister are of sound doctrine and in good standing. And on that basis they will attend Lord's Supper with another congregation. I know that, at least in some URCs there's an interview and then something goes back to the home consistory to say that so-and-so attended Lord's Supper here. I guess the difference is that, historically speaking, we did that upfront. We didn't tell the home consistory after the fact that someone attended, but rather, beforehand, and put the responsibility upon the brother and sister to get the attestation, so that there is that clear connection that those who are ordained to supervise those attending the Lord's Supper, hear a testimony to their faithfulness. These are practical matters that need to be talked about and worked on, but I am fully confident that such matters could be worked out.

Elder Howard Lubbers:

Good evening and thanks for your presentation. I have one question on what you wrote on the bottom of page 12 [p. 30 in this book], with regard to the states that we are in, and the very last part, where it says: "and of justification by grace through faith wherein we are enabled not to sin." So is it your position that, possibly on this side of the grave we are able to not sin, and even possibly to lead a perfect life?

Dr. Van Raalte:

That's not our position. Even the best works of the saints are tainted with sin. We know this of ourselves by experience: you do some good work, and then afterwards, what happens? You pat yourself on the back and all of a sudden you are smitten with remorse because you have taken glory for yourself. So, even the best works of the saints are still filled with sin. But we must not diminish the power of the work of the Holy Spirit in regeneration who does enable us not to sin, and "begin in this life the eternal Sabbath," that rest from sin. It's a beginning, it's not a completion. And we could say that the sentence is a little bit of a short form because to "justification by grace through faith" you probably should add: plus the gift of the Spirit in sanctification, and then say we are enabled not to sin. Okay?

Moderator:

Rev. Najapfour –

Rev. Najapfour:

Thank you so much. I appreciate very much your dialogue, and I only have one question. How would you comment on those who say that we are to view our covenant children as elect, or born again, and therefore, by implication, we do not need to call them to repentance, or faith? I often hear that comment, and I am curious as to how you would respond to that. Thank you.

Dr. Van Vliet:

Brother, I think I understood your question, could you just repeat it again, or sum it up? Just to make sure we understand.

Rev. Najapfour:

Yes. How do you respond to, let's say families, who would say to you, well my child is a covenant child, and therefore I am to view my child as elect, or born again, and therefore by implication there is no need for me to present the gospel to my child, after all, he or she is already elect, by virtue perhaps of God's covenant. Thank you.

Dr. Van Vliet:

I would point [out], brother . . . if such parents spoke like that, I would say: were you listening when the Form for Baptism was read, when your child was baptized? For, right from the beginning of the Form it was said: "First, we and our children are conceived and born in sin and therefore are by nature children of wrath, so that we cannot enter the kingdom of God, unless we are born again." It does not say that the sacrament is administered because your child is born again, it says, clearly, unless we are born again. There the Form says, this is what has to happen. But we cannot give that rebirth to ourselves. Only God, through the power of the Holy Spirit, John 3, can give us regeneration. And therefore we have these promises as well. Clearly, covenant children have to be called to faith, called to repentance.

Rev. Najapfour:

Amen.

Dr. Van Raalte:

I'd like to add one thing. A good number of our churches have used Ted Tripp's video series *Shepherding a Child's Heart*. And if there's anything that's clear from Ted Tripp's video series, it's that you are as a parent seeking to bring out, to reach the heart of your child. You are not just conforming them to some moral obedience, you want them to come to a living faith in the Lord Jesus Christ. And we've all benefited from that, and that's what we teach. I can't say that everyone always teaches it exactly right, or the same, or whatever, but that call is vitally important. We are looking for that when we bring our young people through Catechism classes. I mean, I know some colleague ministers who say, I don't just stand there and teach my class, I look them in the eye and say, why are you here? What are we doing? You are here to come to a mature expression of your faith, to make public profession of faith. That's your answer to God's promise of baptism. And, you know, as consistory, when they come for an exam, we ask them, do you trust in the Lord Jesus Christ for the forgiveness of all your sins? We need to know these things. And, yes, so our children, we need to teach them those things as well.

Moderator:
I see brother Benjamins, and brother Lankheet.

Elder John Benjamins:
Thank you brothers. My question is, you had mentioned that every two months at your Lord's Supper, your form, we know kind of distinguishes. And I know you also do church discipline. I know it is exercised, the keys of the kingdom. How would you say the keys of the kingdom are used in your preaching? I need you to explain just a little bit about that. And, to kind of connect that, what do you think of "discriminating preaching?" I am sure you've heard of that phrase. How would you look at "discriminating preaching?" Those are my questions, thank you.

Dr. Van Vliet:
I think that we tried to get at this matter when we said that, in point 5 on page 14 [pages 19–20 in this book]:

> In addition much can be gained by emphasizing the two parts of the covenant: promise and obligation (Gen 17:4, 9; *Form for Baptism*). If the preacher emphasizes both parts, in the right order and in a balanced way, his congregation will not walk away with the impression that one is automatically

saved simply because he is baptized. Furthermore, the obligation is, in the first place, a call to trust the LORD and believe in the covenant promises he has given, and then, flowing out of that to also live a life of holiness (LD 23-24, 32-33).

It's true that the term "discriminatory preaching" is not one that, you know, we use all of the time, it's not part of our common lingo. But, what is part of our practice, and [also] wholeheartedly [so], is that you need to preach everything that's in the Scripture; you need to preach the two parts of the covenant and do that heartfeltly, do that powerfully, and that will discriminate. The Lord will work his [redemptive] work through that kind of preaching.

Dr. Van Raalte:

I can do this briefly. When I grew up, I don't remember the minister ever distinguishing and saying, now for you who are elect, I have this message, and for you who are not, I have that message. In fact I don't think a Canadian Reformed minister has ever done that, as far as I know. I don't do *that*. But in preaching, I love those opportunities when I know that there are unbelievers in the congregation, from outside, people who don't profess to be Christians, and I can address them in the preaching, and say, do you believe in the Lord Jesus Christ, look what the gospel says, and you have to believe in him. But then again, I say that to my congregation when I am preaching (I no longer have a congregation to serve actively now, but I still preach all the time). They need the call to faith. If the preaching of the gospel doesn't call God's people to faith, it lulls them to sleep. So, discriminating? Not in the sense that we would say, I have this message for that part of the congregation, and that message for that part, but in terms of saying, at times, if you don't believe in the Lord Jesus Christ, you need to. You don't just assume all your congregation does. Sometimes we also pray for those present who haven't accepted this message. So, yeah, it happens.

Moderator:
Rev. Lankheet and then Rev. Van Eeden Petersman

Rev. Lankheet:
So, brother Bouwers maybe just a little clarification? The question time is about covenant and election and the issues in the paper, or can we go more broadly? Questions were asked about the Lord's Supper. I am not quite sure if you want to keep it focused on the paper and the topics?

Moderator:
Largely, yes.

Rev. Lankheet:
Largely yes. Then I think I'll . . . but just let me make this observation. I am personally living now in Canada, being an American, who never knew a real-live Canadian Reformed person until—well that is not true, brother Den Hollander was in my Greek class at Calvin College, so I did know a real-life Canadian Reformed person. I don't think I knew that at the time. But the biggest concern for me is not the theology. Every time I hear a Canadian Reformed pastor preach, every time I hear a lecture at the Seminary, the Theological College in Hamilton, wow, we're on the same page, there's unity. My concern is on the practical issues of day-to-day congregational life, frequency of Lord's Supper, the Forms . . . So we're talking about all the unity. But personally, I think a lot of us are concerned, if we go for unity, are we going to be spending the next ten, twenty years having all this restudying about frequency of communion, what kind

of forms, attestations, women voting in congregational meetings, all this sort of culture-stuff in the church that we are gradually figuring out in one way, and that the Canadian Reformed Churches have, by and large, another kind of culture? And are we—rather than arguing about our main theology, the *Three Forms of Unity*—going to take a lot of time on the minutia and the other things? So maybe a forum, or questions on those other things sometime would be good. Because I really think that's where the rubber's going to hit the road more than covenant, and election, and Mosaic covenant, and all that. It's going to be the practical issues: *Book of Praise,* Genevan tunes, common cup, individual cup—those are the things that are potentially going to be more decisive, in my personal opinion.

Moderator:
Alright. We will instruct the committee to take note. Thank you.
Brother Van Eeden Petersman.

Rev. Van Eeden Petersman:
Thank you. In the opening of Dr. Godfrey and Dr. Venema's letter, on page 2, item 3 [pages 4–5 in this book] was not addressed in your responses. Would you briefly explain how the CanRCs regard the decisions of recent URCNA synods on these topics, concerning justification and election? I note at your 2013 synod in Carman, there were three churches that wrote letters questioning the decisions that we've come to in the URC. The debate for this night is in the interest of exploring possible barriers to federative unity, and so I wonder if a united federation would be seen to maintain the important stand that we took to affirm and articulate our confessional commitment to the Reformed doctrine of justification?

Is that clear? Chiefly the question is, would you explain briefly how the CanRCs regard the decisions of recent URC synods, particularly the *Report on Justification*?

Dr. Van Vliet:
The question of historical background? It's probably important to understand that, going back to 1944, the birth of the Vrijgemaakt, or here on this side, the Canadian Reformed, had to do with an issue of being bound to certain statements beyond what were in the *Three Forms of Unity*. And when that was pressed, that's when the difficulties began. Now, so we've tended to be very careful about that. And if you've followed Canadian Reformed history and synods, we're not in the habit of making a lot of statements on this or that; we are cautious about that. Why? Because we are always reminding ourselves that at the end of the day, what are you going to do with discipline? Right? So, if you make a certain statement at a synod, are you going to discipline on that, yes or no? Clearly in our Form of Subscription we have said that on confessional matters, there will be discipline if there is transgression. So, always with that in mind, we can talk, we can debate things, but . . . So, now as URCNA you have subscription to *Confessions*, you have *Doctrinal Affirmations*, you have *Pastoral Advice*. Is there one more?

Moderator:
There could be.

Dr. Van Vliet
So our Synod Carman has said to our Deputies in our Committee for Church Unity: look into that, talk about that, we need to figure out where this is going.

But to your question about the Reformed doctrine of justification, I hope this evening has demonstrated that we are one with you, brothers, in wanting to firmly defend the doctrine of justification in all of its purity.

But there will [need to] be discussion on all of these categories [of statements] and how that links to the *Form of Subscription*. I suppose you may have had those discussions among yourselves as well.

Dr. Van Raalte:

A brief addition? You mentioned three churches, that's three out of about 55; they're writing to Synod. The question is, what does Synod do with it? I mean, we could have a minister that teaches a very aberrant doctrine, but that doesn't fault us. The problem is whether we discipline him or not, right? I am not saying that this is a matter of discipline, but the fact is that the Synod did not accede to the concerns of these churches. And it doesn't represent the majority of the churches. So, keep that in mind. And then the other thing, the Nine Points [Synod Schererville, 2007] and then the Fifteen Points [Synod London, 2010], as they came forward, some of them were at first not appreciated by Canadian Reformed consistories. But it turned out, and they realized that soon enough, that they were reading them against the background of 1944 and not against the background of *Federal Vision*. When you read them in their proper context, they are appreciated. And it seems to be that, by and large, these are appreciated among us. And certainly I would want to, and I think I can speak for all of my colleagues at the Seminary, definitely want to preserve the free grace of justification in whatever way that needs to be done.

Moderator:

I recognize Rev. Marcusse. But I have a question for the chairman [of Synod]. We had agreed to sort of an open-ended [format], but we are at the order of the day. So, what is your advice?

Rev. Bradd Nymeyer, Chairman of Synod:
By my watch we began the colloquium at 7:20. That leaves an hour for the colloquium, that's 8:20. We said *no more than* an hour for questions. I would entertain a motion to extend the order of the day.

Moved, supported, carried.

Rev. Ed Marcusse:
I want to thank the brothers, all the brothers up there, for coming and doing this here tonight. And I want to say that I think the talk here tonight has really reinforced where my thinking has been going. And that is that our differences are not in our theology. I hear you explain these various points and I like what I am hearing. Our differences lie in our practices. And I want to repeat, or slightly repeat the things two of the men have already said.

Your answer to that question on parents who assume that their child is saved simply because they are part of the covenant; your answer is exactly right. And yet let me also tell you my personal experience with the Canadian Reformed Church. A dozen years ago we were serving a church in Canada, and this was right when the whole idea of union started coming up and the recommendation from Synod was, you have to meet with them, you have to get to know them, we have to get to know one another. So I went back with that to my elders, and my elders said, yeah that's great, that's a good idea, let's do that. We met across the table with the Canadian Reformed Church. At their invitation we went to them and they sat on that side of the table and we—I and my elders—sat on this side of the table, and the discussion went along. But I remember asking them, I myself asked this, and so maybe I could have said it in a better way, a more understandable way, maybe we talked past one another. But I asked them this, I said, how do you evangelize your children? How do you preach the gospel to your children?

And it was this dead silent in there. They looked at one another, shrugged their shoulders, and there was no response. Until the minister, the minister himself, finally said that our children are told that you are already saved, now go out and live it. And that broke my heart. Because that will kill the church quicker than any other thing. And that is my concern with this whole process.

I lived in a "former life." And that's our codeword for coming out of a previous denomination. That was a dying church. And the Lord, by his grace, gave us this federation through blood, sweat, and tears. And I do not want to go back to a dying church.

That's my concern. And that's my experience. And I hope you can tell me that was one rogue, strange teaching. But none of the elders there could give us a reason. I have a copy of that minister's sermon from Peter, that said you are saved by your baptism. It is obviously what he taught, over and over and over again. That's my concern.

Dr. Van Vliet:

Thank you brother. I will try to step through what you've said. So the question was to the group of elders there and the minister, "How do you evangelize your children?" That's the way you phrased the question. I can understand why that threw the brothers. Because if the question had been phrased, how do you preach the gospel to your children? Or how do you impress on them the fact that they need to believe and they shouldn't just, you know, assume that, well, I was baptized and however I live, it will be okay in the end? But when the question was phrased, "How do you evangelize your children?" [Well,] evangelism, in the minds of those brothers, is probably associated with speaking to, preaching to those who are outside the covenant, who are presumably pagans. Then they would have been thinking, yes, but these are covenant children. The Lord has given them a great privilege in being covenant children, children of believers, and they have the sacrament, they have the promises that are signed and sealed in the sacrament, they have the obligation, also the call to believe and to [live out] the new obedience, as the Form says. So, I can see that the phrasing of the question threw them off because of the terminology: evangelize.

But as you rephrased it yourself, then, that's helpful: how do we preach the gospel to our children? Well, of course, we have to preach the gospel to our children.

Now then your next question was about when the minister finally spoke and said: we tell our children they are saved, now go out and live it. I am assuming that's a direct quote. I don't know, but I will assume that. I think the way that you would need to work with that is to say: Okay now brother, what do you *mean* by that? Do you mean that each and every child that is baptized, by the very fact that he's been baptized, has been saved? Isn't that an *ex opera operato* type of theology? You would need to press him on that. And I would hope (because I wasn't in your circumstance, but I would hope) that had you pressed him like that, he would have backed off and phrased things differently. But I don't know what happened there, in that room, okay? But yeah, so leave that for a beginning [comment].

Rev. Christopher Folkerts:

Again, thank you brothers for being here and it's really good to hear your answers. And again my question is on the practical side of things. I was born and raised in Canada and had the privilege of going to a Canadian Reformed school. And in my experience, which is not just limited to where I lived, but [includes] talking to other youth from the URCNA (in Alberta, for example), we came to see that there seemed to be a lot of worldliness amongst the youth in the Canadian Reformed, a lot of partying and drinking, to the extent that I wasn't invited to their parties. No, seriously though, this was something that really grieved me, and I wasn't going to put up with it. So the question is, as I began to wrestle with that, it seemed like this was a result of what we have called a hyper-covenantalism: my children are born within the covenant, therefore everything is good. They might even sow their wild oats, but when they are thirty, forty, they'll come back. And so I guess my question is—again this is a matter of perception—but is there, and in trying to listen to the other comments that have been made, are we saying to our children, are you saying to your children, are the preachers saying to the children of the church: you need to be converted, and you need to live a holy life, and is there—like I echo the sentiment that our [Heritage] Reformed [fraternal] delegate was speaking to us about: a call to piety. And I think that's well from the URC churches. I know we don't live up to our confession either, we don't live up to the Word of God, we fall very short, so I am aware of that too. But what I am anxious to see and hear is, is there within the Canadian Reformed Churches a really heartfelt, robust, gut-wrenching cry to the youth: you need to live a godly life, a pious life, a holy life, a life that shuns sin. And I know our confessions speak about that, and I know here theologically we can all agree on that. But practically, what's going on in the life of the Canadian Reformed youth in particular, how are they being brought to that holiness? Thank you.

Dr. Van Raalte:

Well, the last question, and this one, in terms of being anecdotal, are similar, in that anecdotes are always hard to deal with. But it's—I'll be honest—it's been my sense that this is something that we needed to improve on. I can remember, growing up, and the minister we had would actually stop the sermon and say . . . "You in the back over there, wake up!" and somebody had to poke the person. And, actually, I was the little kid sitting in the front once, and I woke up to his finger pointing right at me: this is for you too!

It scared me out of ever sleeping again. My cure for not sleeping now is, I preach instead.

This grieves me as well, as a pastor I've gone into a bar and taken kids out. And one of them was in my pre-confession class, and I said, look, you've got to make a choice right now. If you want to go back in, you are out of my pre-confession class. Because this place, it wasn't just a friendly-have-a-beer, it wasn't a good place. And these sorts of concerns, yeah I understand them because I know what was going on when I grew up. My children are younger right now, they are just, you know, starting to come to that age. God has blessed them, the ones that are at home, to be very godly, and receive these things, and to love the Lord. But there are going to come times when they are challenged and then I have to step up to the plate. It may be that in some cases the parents do think this way: it's a stage, they'll snap out of it. I've preached against that. The elders—the church I was pastoring was in Winnipeg—as elders we knew that there was a hockey tournament, the young people were drinking. Stuff went wrong, some of them came back for Sunday, some of them didn't. We sat down with a group of eight of them and we had it out and said: is this the Christian way, and should they live this way? So what more can we do, than keep working on it, cry out from the pulpit, deal with them individually, and try to stir up parents to care about it more. I don't think things like that should prevent us from church unity. But where, let's say, a neighbouring pastor or elder became aware of it, don't just say, oh, there they go! But come and share that with your brother elder or pastor in the Canadian Reformed Church and help us.

Moderator:
Thank you.

Brothers to my left [the URC brethren, Dr. Godfrey and Dr.

Venema]. Do you have any comments to make? Any final words? I don't see any further questions coming from the floor.

Dr Godfrey:
We've enjoyed this part of the discussion very much. [laughter]

Dr. Van Vliet:
I would like to add something to what was just said.

Here at this synod, I had a discussion with a URC minister struggling with similar things in his own congregation. So, as my colleague has said, this is all the more reason that we need each other.

We've heard a number of addresses here [saying] that Satan is out to attack the church. And we need to help each other and stand together, to resist all of his attacks. Whether that's among the older, whether that's among the youth. And we need to look at it in that way: let's help each other address those problems. We all agree about what's wrong.

Dr. Van Raalte:
Okay, in closing?

Moderator:
Yes, sure. Do you have some final remarks, and then I will ask these [the URC] brothers as well.

Dr. Van Raalte:
Okay, I thought about these closing remarks [ahead of time and made some notes in preparation].[1]

---

1. The audio of the remainder of the address was not recorded. Dr. Van Raalte has provided a reconstruction of his concluding remarks based on his notes.

I would like to close my remarks by emphasizing that all of our careful theological constructions of covenant theology are intended to illuminate the person and work of our Lord Jesus Christ. They should not make him obscure but glorify him in all his saving work and help us see him in all the Scriptures. We should do our work in the spirit of the request those Greeks made of the disciples in John 12:21, "Sir, we would see Jesus!" Our theologizing should help us see him in all of Scripture, for he himself explained to the two men on the road to Emmaus "all that was said in the Scriptures concerning himself" (Luke 24:27). Indeed, he had earlier said, "These are the Scriptures that testify about me" (John 5:39). A chapter later John records his saying, "The work God requires is to believe the one he has sent" (John 6:29). Let our theology serve this call to faith! Paul said that, "Jesus Christ has become for us wisdom from God, that is, our righteousness and holiness and redemption (1 Cor 1:30). Thus Paul knew "nothing but Christ and him crucified" (1 Cor 2:2).

Though we have debated some finer points, in the end the purpose is to make manifest our unity in doctrine which itself manifests our unity in Christ, in him as the Unique Person. And we are motivated in our covenant theology to give clarity and power to our preaching of Christ. We believe he took the covenant curse and so destroyed death, supplied the active obedience required in the covenant and so brought to light life and immortality through the gospel (2 Tim 1:10). His resurrection was a reward for his obedience within the covenant. He merited that. Thus he brings us to the new creation, with no more sin or curse, with immortality and imperishability, for Christ is also our God. He completed the work the Father gave him to do on earth

(John 17:4). He himself, in his person, is the consummation of the covenant. He is Immanuel, God with us, so the very centre of the covenant is found in him. Let us give him the glory.

5

A Common Covenant Theology?
Thoughts on the CanRC/URC Colloquium

DANIEL R. HYDE

On November 13, 2012,[1] I addressed the North American Presbyterian and Reformed Council (NAPARC) with a speech entitled, "From Reformed Dream to Reformed Reality: The Problem and Possibility of Reformed Church Unity."[2] In it I sought to further the "Reformed Dream"[3] of one of my fathers in the faith, Dr. W. Robert Godfrey, to see more and more unity between Reformed and Presbyterian denominations and

---

1. This chapter was originally published online on The Aquila Report http://theaquilareport.com/a-common-covenant-theology/J. It also appeared in Christian Renewal Vol. 32.14 (June 25, 2014), pp. 14–16. Republished here with permission.
2. See http://theaquilareport.com/from-reformed-dream-to-reformed-reality-the-problem-and-possibility-of-reformed-church-unity/
3. See http://www.modernreformation.org/default.php?page=article display&var2=123

federations. In response to it at least one minister wrote in his denominational publication that I was "another dreamer."[4]

As I write, the Synod of my federation, the United Reformed Churches in North America, is meeting. One of the perpetual agenda items we have faced since Synod 2001 is uniting together with the Canadian Reformed Churches. This has proven to be daunting and difficult for many reasons. From my side of the ecclesiastical fence, the biggest issue I have had over the years relates to covenant theology and in particular how it relates to the gospel promise of justification.

On the agenda for Synod 2014 is a colloquium between two URC professors (Cornel Venema and Bob Godfrey) and two CanRC professors (Ted Van Raalte and Jason Van Vliet) on the doctrine of covenant in Scripture and the Three Forms of Unity. The goal is to explore commonality, differences, and/or perceived differences. Prior to Synod we were given a helpful fifteen page interaction between these brothers.[5] On the basis of this interaction (which I will cite and interact with below), I want to say the following:

First, insofar as Drs. Van Raalte and Van Vliet represent a "typical" CanRC understanding (p. 1),[6] I am happy and satisfied with the main contours of their discussion. These are conscientious brothers who are laboring to be confessionally Reformed men in our a-confessional age. I respect that. Their writing is the clearest expression of how CanRC covenant

4. See http://standardbearer.rfpa.org/articles/another-dreamer
5. See chapters 1 & 2 of this book.
6. Editor's note: Rev. Hyde here is referring to statement in a one-page covering letter drafted by CERCU for the URCNA, and not included in this book. The letter stated, "In the material that is attached, two able and respected professors from each of our federations have served the churches by interacting with each other and then articulating 'a' typical URC perspective of these matters and 'a' typical Canadian Reformed perspective."

theology relates to justification that I personally have read. I hope my fathers and brothers in the URCNA see that.

Appreciation

For example, concerning Adam pre-fall, they are not afraid to speak of "God's covenanted reward . . . by way of Adam's perfect obedience" (p. 14). They speak of the fact that what Adam would have received had he been obedient as meritum ex pacto, that is, "a reward for his obedience within the terms of his relationship with God" (p. 14).

For example, concerning the second Adam and justification, they unequivocally affirm "that Christ alone fully merited our salvation and that God imputes to his elect both the active and passive obedience of Christ" (p. 15). They say that as it relates to justification "law and gospel are antithetical concepts" (p. 15). They agree that we must "affirm [. . .] the distinction and disjunction between the pre-fall and post-fall situations. Indeed, we affirm a radical discontinuity that must be strongly emphasized so as to avoid Pelagian errors" (p. 16). They speak of faith as it relates to justification "rely[ing] entirely upon, and accept[ing], the free gift of Christ's perfect righteousness, satisfaction and holiness" and of faith as it relates to sanctification "produc[ing] the fruits of good works" (pp. 20–21).

For example, concerning covenant and election they speak, albeit in a very qualified sense, of "a certain duality in the covenant" as it relates to believers and unbelievers, elect and reprobate within the historical administration of the covenant of grace (p. 18). They speak of the reality that some in the covenant are so "in a merely external and superficial manner" while others are so "genuinely . . . from the heart in true dedication" (p. 19). They speak of hypocrites who are merely in the church, or covenant, while not being of it (p. 21).

For example, concerning preaching to the baptized, they speak of the priority of calling our baptized children first to faith and then to holiness that flows out of faith (p. 20).

Small Differences and Questions

Second, it's obvious that there are differences in terminology and differences in how covenant theology is preached and played out in the life of the local congregation, given the living historical consciousness of the CanRC (1944 Vrijmaking) as well as the diversity represented within the URCNA. I believe, though, that the differences of such terminology and some of the nuances of our theological expressions may be discussed intramurally as brothers in the Lord and co-laborers in the gospel. My two brothers do not use the exact and precise terminology that I use, but the substance is the same per above. I could say the same, no doubt, between fellow URCNA ministers and myself. I think one of the reasons for this is the difference in speaking strictly confessionally as distinct from more broadly theologically. In light of this, I would like to demonstrate to my brothers and our broader ecclesiastical audiences that we can discuss such intramural questions in the spirit of iron sharpening iron. Let me offer a few, to which Drs. Van Raalte and Van Vliet will respond in the next issue of Christian Renewal.

Regarding Adam's creation in the image of God and its relation to the pre-fall covenant, Godfrey and Venema cite Heidelberg Catechism, Q&A 6, which goes on to say the purpose of this was "so that" (German, *aus dass*; Latin, *ut* with the subjunctive verbs *cognosceret, diligeret,* and *viveret*) Adam might know God, love him, and "live with him in eternal happiness." Godfrey and Venema cite this as evidence within the Catechism itself of an understanding that Adam was created for "something more," which is one of the ideas incorporated later into the concept of a covenant of life or works. Van Raalte and Van Vliet take issue with this and say it is taken out of context given that what the Catechism is dealing with "is not in the context of Adam doing good works but in the context of having been created good . . . Adam was created in true righteousness, not that he had to earn it" (p. 10). My question for my brothers is why the false choice? Can Q&A 6 not be saying both? In fact, Zacharius Ursinus himself, chief author of the Catechism, said it was a "both/and" situation with Adam. In his lectures Ursinus took up the objection that "the felicity and happiness of man . . . are properties or conditions with and in which he was created . . . therefore they are not the ends for which man was created" (Ursinus, Commentary on the Heidelberg Catechism, p. 29). Ursinus' answer was that the properties of Adam's being created in the image of God was not only his "form" (*forme*) but also his "end" (*finis*) in which he was to continue. He went on to say that the question was not only about the "what" (*qualis*) of Adam but also about "for what" (*ad quid*) he was created.[7]

Regarding the issue of the relationship between law and gospel after justification in the life of believers, my brothers know this has been one of the thorny issues of theology since at least from the time of the era of high orthodoxy (ca. 1640ff.). Anthony Burgess said relating law and gospel was "one of the hardest tasks in all divinity."[8] Van Raalte and Van Vliet echo Scripture (John 3:36; 2 Thess. 1:8; Rev. 3:14–22) and confession (Canons of Dort 5.14) in saying that the gospel is to be obeyed and that the gospel threatens. I do not disagree that this is what is said, but what precisely is meant? Would it be helpful to distinguish law and gospel: redemptive historically/theologically, properly/improperly, and narrowly/broadly considered? Granting the limitations of this particular colloquium, I think some more nuance would help further brothers like me on this side of the fence.

---

7. Zacharias Ursinus, *Corpus Doctrinae Orthodoxae*, [1616], p. 34.
8. Anthony Burgess, *Vindiciae Legis*, p. 5.

Regarding how preaching is affected by covenant theology, I would appreciate some further clarity. I appreciate the focus on the two outcomes that arise among those within the covenant of grace per Scripture: blessing and cursing. Yet, there is a follow-up paragraph that states "there is more than a difference in outcomes, there is also a difference in the way that individual believers live *within* the covenant" (p. 19; emphasis original). The brothers go on to contrast those who "merely 'go through the motions' and live within the covenant in a merely external and superficial manner" with those who "live within the covenant genuinely . . . from the heart in true dedication to, and with fellowship with, the Lord." (p. 19). I'm assuming there is a misprint here as I would never say those who go through the motions externally and superficially are "believers." Am I missing something? Or is this a reference to believers who are backslidden, lukewarm, or slothful and who need to be revived? Further, in the final paragraph the comment is made in caution that we do not say "church members must at a certain point in time receive the Lord Jesus Christ in some kind of special conversion experience" (p. 22). Delete "special" and "experience" and would you agree that everyone within the covenant is called to conversion by repenting of sin and placing their faith in Jesus Christ? Is the promise of Christ and the command to repent and believe also proclaimed within the covenant promiscuously and indiscriminately and not just to those out there apart from the covenant (Canons of Dort 2.5)?

Do the CanRCs and URCs have a common covenant theology? . . . I believe the answer is yes on the main outline . . .

In conclusion, do the CanRCs and URCs have a common covenant theology? If the two presentations made in this colloquium are truly representative of both the Three Forms of Unity as well as our ministers, then I believe the answer is yes on the main outline, while in terms of the details, expressions, nuances, and practicalities of preaching and living out this doctrine the answer is, we have work to do *inter nos*.

In the end, I remain a dreamer.

6

Response to Rev. Daniel Hyde's, "A Common Covenant Theology?"

THEODORE G. VAN RAALTE AND JASON P. VAN VLIET

Introduction

To begin with, we want to thank Rev. Daniel Hyde for the positive and brotherly fashion in which he commented on our theses concerning the doctrine of the covenant. Our original document was divided into two parts: the pre-fall covenant (covenant of works) and the covenant of grace. Since Rev. Hyde's questions also fall into those two categories, we'll continue the same format.

Pre-fall covenant (covenant of works)

1. Do we raise a false dilemma in our concerns about Venema and Godfrey's use of QA 6?

We grant that doctrinally no dilemma needs to be made between Adam's blessedness as a state in which he was created and his blessedness as a thing to which he was aimed by God (an "end"). In this regard we agree completely with Ursinus and with Hyde.

However, we still maintain that QA 6 as such does not speak of "something more" (Hyde's phrase). Nor does Ursinus at this point in his commentary. He writes, rather, that Adam's happy communion with God, etc., was "for this end that he might forever remain such" (Ursinus, *Commentary on the Heidelberg Catechism*, p. 29).

We affirm entirely that God's intention was to bring Adam to an immutable fellowship, a state wherein he would no longer be able to sin. However, we avoid reading into our catechism the doctrine that Adam had to earn or merit a higher state. Though versions of such theological constructions are not forbidden, we wish to avoid binding one another to them since they are not required either by the express statements or the implications of our confessions.

2. What is meant by the gospel needing to be "obeyed" and the gospel "threatening" its hearers? Should we distinguish various senses of the law/gospel distinction?

We added these remarks not to diminish in any way the complete antithesis of law and gospel in the matter of justification. Rather, we were inviting discussion on the role of the law and the gospel in the Christian's life. That is: should we as Christians find the gospel to be pure sweetness whereas the law is always a goad, a whip, and a heavy yoke? Since this came up only briefly in the colloquium herewith our thanks to Rev. Hyde for raising it again.

As we had noted, Scripture speaks of "those who do not obey the gospel of Christ" being punished at the last day (2 Thess 1:8). In Romans 10:16 this clearly refers to those who do not obey the command of the gospel to repent from sin and believe in Christ. In First Peter 4:17 the phrase "disobey the "gospel" parallels "disobey the word" in 2:8 and 3:1. Primarily the meaning appears to be the same as in Romans 10:16—the call to faith. But we would add that repeatedly in our lives as Christians we must repent of disobeying the gospel by not believing, not just of disobeying the law. Continually, we need to appropriate our reconciliation with God (see 2 Cor 5:20; Rev 3:3).

But we should say more, for the implication of believing the gospel of salvation in Christ is to live a life that demonstrates such reconciliation. The bond between such faith and life is very intricate, for the Apostle Paul once summarized his ministry of "fully proclaiming the gospel of Christ," as leading the Gentiles to "obey" God (Rom 15:18–19). Similarly, he wrote twice of the "law of Christ," which he said he was "under" and we ought to "fulfill" by bearing one another's burdens in love (1 Cor 9:21; Gal 6:2). Paul the believer expressed high praise for the law (Rom 7:12,14,16,22,25).

The "law of Christ" is God's law, as given to believers who are by grace in Christ freed from its destructive power (Rom 8:1–4). It is the law of life, loved and delighted in by the church (Psalms 19, 119), and governing the obedience that ought to accompany one's confession of the gospel of Christ (2 Cor 9:13). It itself certainly is not the gospel, but only the gospel enables us to love it and begin to obey it, and the gospel lays upon us this "light and easy yoke" as an implication of calling Christ our Lord (Matt 7:21; 11:30; Gal 5:13–15).

There are also commands that may rightly be called "gospel commands" because they flow out of the gospel as implications of it and apply only to believers. These are "in accord with sound doctrine" (1 Tim 1:10–11; Titus 2:1). For instance, the gospel, not the law, put the apostle to the Gentiles under obligation (1 Cor 9:16). Believers are warned strongly not to be unequally yoked with unbelievers (2 Cor 6:14-7:1). Strong admonitions are reserved for the church in Hebrews 10:28-9, 12:25, and Revelation 3:3,16,19. The threats in the new covenant are weightier than those in the old, for the church has received so much more through the gospel

(Heb 10:28-9). The flip side of the gospel's sweet promises are the threats of condemnation for those who do not believe (John 3:36) and who do not live in accordance with the gospel (Heb 6:4-8; 1 Tim 1:8-11).

According to our catechism, true repentance includes a "love and delight to live according to the will of God in all good works" (QA 90). For this reason the lengthier treatment of the law in our catechism is within the framework of the gospel, as evidence of our thankfulness (QA 86-115). Such thankfulness grows out of the unity of the work of the Father, Son, and Holy Spirit (QA 86). It includes a continual striving to do better (QA 115).

Rev. Hyde wonders about using various distinctions. One can indeed appeal to the wider and narrower senses of terms, such as speaking of the law in its accusing power as the naked law, abstracted from its proper or wider redemptive context (*nuda lex*; see I. John Hesselink, *Calvin's Concept of the Law*, p. 158). But perhaps the simplest approach is to distinguish the three functions of the law: accusing; civil; and normative uses, while noting the complete dependence of the latter on the gospel.

Covenant of grace

Concerning the covenant, which the LORD made with Abraham and his descendants, and still graciously extends to us and our children, Rev. Hyde asks us two basic questions. We'll paraphrase each question and provide an answer.

1. Are hypocrites "believers" or was that a typo in your original submission?

In short it was the unfortunate result of putting a document through numerous revisions. The sentence in question was: "there is more than a difference in outcomes, there is also a difference in the way that individual believers live within the covenant." That sentence should have read: ". . . a difference in the way that individuals live within the covenant." There are hypocrites in the covenant community, but hypocrites are not genuine believers.

2. Would you agree that everyone within the covenant is called to conversion by repenting of sin and placing their faith in Jesus Christ, even if their conversion is not marked by some kind of special, extraordinary experience?

Yes, we would agree. The Canons of Dort affirm that the promise of the gospel ought to be "proclaimed universally and without discrimination to all peoples and all men… together with the command to repent and believe." Not only do we agree with the Canons, but we understand "all peoples and all men" in the plain sense of the phrase: everyone, both within and outside of the covenant of grace. Furthermore, the Form for Baptism speaks of the need for covenant children to be "born again." And each time again, the Form for Lord's Supper reminds us to seriously examine ourselves as to whether we are indeed continuing in faith and repentance. (See especially the sections on "Self-Examination" and "Invitation and Admonition.")

Summary

As the colloquium with Drs. Venema and Godfrey already indicated, and as this further exchange with Rev. Hyde confirms, the URCNA and CanRC share essentially the same covenant theology. To be sure, there are differences of nuance and terminology. However, those differences not only exist between our two federations, but they also exist within our respective federations. Moreover, the distinctive nuances can certainly be discussed among us, *inter nos*, as Rev. Hyde suggests.

We are brothers and our churches are still on the road to greater unity. In short, we share your dream, brother.

7

Postponement or Progress? Personal reflections on Synod Visalia 2014

Jason P. Van Vliet

Synod Visalia 2014 of the United Reformed Churches of North America began with a prayer service on the evening of June 2, and finished with a flurry of decisions on the evening of June 5.[1] In addition to the two fraternal delegates from the Canadian Reformed Churches, Rev. W. Den Hollander and Rev. C. Vandervelde, Dr. Ted Van Raalte and I, also CanRC, were invited to participate in a special colloquium, or discussion, on the doctrine of the covenant. Allow me to reflect on some of the things I experienced there.

A Colloquium on Covenant
At a recent meeting between the CERCU (Committee for

1. Originally published in *Christian Renewal* 32.15 (July 16, 2014), pp. 5, 17, 20. A more extended version appeared in *Clarion* 63.14 (July 18, 2014), pp. 350–54. Reprinted with permission.

Ecumenical Relations and Church Unity) of the URC and the CCU (Co-ordinators for Church Unity) of the CanRC, the topic of the covenant generated enough discussion that the two committees decided to invite four professors, Drs. R. Godfrey & C. Venema (URC) and Drs. T. Van Raalte & J. Van Vliet (CanRC) to have a colloquium about this topic on the floor of synod.

So, what was gained? I'll do my best to capture some highlights. A helpful insight came almost immediately from Dr. Godfrey who pointed out that the URCNA, with a large number of its congregations in the USA, is much more "Presbyterianized" (to use his term) in certain doctrinal and church political (i.e., church order) aspects. This is because the dominant form of Reformed faith in the USA is not continental, or Dutch, Reformed with its Three Forms of Unity, but rather British-Scottish Presbyterianism which adheres to the Westminster Standards. Now it is true that both the URC and CanRC subscribe to the Three Forms of Unity; however, some in the URC are quite familiar with the Westminster Standards and are more likely to use terminology found in those standards such as covenant of works and covenant of grace, or visible and invisible church.

We can discuss the pros and cons of various terms, but let's begin by asking the other: "What do you really mean? What are you driving at?" And let's not assume from the outset that just because someone else uses a different term that he necessarily means a different thing. Both in preparing for and participating in the colloquium, it became evident that if we listen well to what lies at the heart of the other party's concern, we discover that we're not that far apart. In fact, even though we may use different terminology and have different emphases, we could conclude that no matters of confessional difference exist between us.

The URCNA has been engaged in a debate over Federal Vision, also at their general synods. One of their key concerns with FV is that within this movement, some tend to blend together justification and sanctification in such a way that good works become part of the means, or instrument, by which we are justified before God. In addition, since many in the URC have long used the distinction between covenant of works and covenant of grace, they have also seen this distinction as being helpful to ensure that justification remains only by faith and only on the basis of Christ's merit.

Members of the CanRC agree that justification is only by faith and only on Christ's merits. However, since they have not been "presbyterianized" to the same degree, the covenant of works and covenant of grace distinction is not used as much in CanRC circles. Of course, the language of "covenant of grace" is found in the Canons of Dort (Art 1.17 and RE 2.2, 4), as well as our Forms for Baptism and Lord's Supper, but the term "covenant of works" is not. Therefore, as Dr. Van Raalte and I pointed out at Synod Visalia, if the concern is protecting the doctrine of justification, then we can also turn to the clear distinction that the Heidelberg Catechism makes between justification (LD 23-24) in which good works cannot contribute even the most miniscule amount (QA 62-63) and sanctification (LD 32-33) in which good works are confessed as the fruit of faith, but not the content of faith. The content of faith is defined elsewhere in LD 7.

Although the term "covenant of works" is not found in any of our confessions, it has a long history in doctrinal textbooks, also those used in continental Reformed circles such as Herman Bavinck's *Reformed Dogmatics*, Louis Berkhof's *Systematic Theology*, and also in the writings of Klaas Schilder. At the same time, there are other terms that have been used as well for the pre-fall covenant: covenant of life, covenant of nature, covenant of favour, covenant of love. Each term has pros and cons which can be discussed, but it is more important that the doctrine of justification is protected from any synergistic notion that we contribute something, indeed anything, toward our righteousness before God. At the same time, we must all remember that via the Form of Subscription we firmly hold each other to Scripture as summarized in the Three Forms of Unity, but beyond that we do not subscribe to terminology or theological structures in dogmatic textbooks.

> we recognize one another's formulations as being within the bounds of our Three Forms of Unity

In the end, though, all involved in the colloquium could agree that in spite of some different articulation and emphasis we recognize one another's formulations as being within the bounds of our Three Forms of Unity.

A Decision about Union

Many delegates to Synod Visalia expressed appreciation for the colloquium. For them it either cleared up, or confirmed, that the two federations are essentially united in how we understand the doctrine of the covenant. However, that brings us back to the question: "If the doctrine of the covenant is not an obstacle, why don't we move ahead in the work toward church union?" Good question, and Synod Visalia had to deal with it.

Concerning the relationship between the URC and CanRC, there was a proposal before Synod to encourage CERCU to work toward stepping ahead into Phase 3A (to begin designing a plan for church union) in two years. This proposal was postponed indefinitely. As I understand it, this means that while the assembly did not disagree with the proposal, it did not agree with it either. Instead, it simply said, "At this time we're not going to take a decision on this particular proposal."

To be as clear as possible, the CanRC relationship with the URC was not postponed indefinitely. In fact, there was another proposal before Synod stating that all the efforts we presently have in order to come to know each other better should continue, and that proposal was adopted. So we're still in Phase 2 – ecclesiastical fellowship. The only thing that was postponed indefinitely was the proposal to encourage CERCU to begin the work that would be necessary to step ahead to Phase 3A.

It's been 20 or more years since discussions between the URC (formerly Independent Reformed) and CanRC began. Some may feel that we're now stalling at Phase 2. Some may be losing patience with the process. Some may be inclined to say, "Let's just live happily together in Phase 2; it's so much easier."

I disagree for two reasons. First, although there was no formal progress in our mutual relationship at Synod Visalia 2014, there has been, and continues to be, significant informal progress. Compared to the last URC Synod I attended, back in London in 2010, there was noticeably more familiarity with, and understanding of, each other. The colloquium, and the way it was received, indicates that good progress is being made in our mutual ability to discuss matters, even intricate doctrinal matters, and come to a consensus. This is something to be deeply grateful for and bodes well for the future.

Second, both in principle and in official decisions, it would seem that our two federations agree that church union is an ideal, albeit very challenging, goal. The URC, for some time already, has had three phases in their ecumenical relations, the third phase being "Church Union." In a slightly different way, the CanRC has indicated the same intention by appointing a Committee for Church Unity (CCU). I could be mistaken but I expect that the URC Phase 3 and the CanRC CCU are in place because of scriptural passages such as John 17:20-21 and Eph. 4:1-3. Those words of our God remain the same as they were 20 years ago when the talks began. It's my impression that there are members in both federations who are convinced in their hearts that Phase 2, or ecclesiastical fellowship, is as far as we can realistically come in this fallen world. But then I would respectfully ask, "Why are Phase 3 and the CCU in our official decisions?" Maybe that's a good topic for another colloquium, or at least a lot of "mini-colloquiums" around our coffee (and consistory) tables. And let us pray that our heavenly Father, whose almighty providential hand guides all things, would bring us to the point where stepping toward Phase 3A does not look like an insurmountable obstacle but rather an edifying opportunity.

Appendix 1: Reflections on the Conclusions of Utrecht

CERCU

The following material was presented to both the URCNA and FRCNA (Free Reformed) Synods in 2014. The hope was that by means of reflection on this report the churches of both federations could receive from one another an expression of what lives in the thinking and practice of our respective churches.

The Conclusions of Utrecht are included for your reference in Appendix 2 of this publication.

The decision of the URCNA Synod Visalia, Acts of Synod Article 26.8 was to conclude for the benefit of the Free Reformed Churches that the [following] report gives faithful expression to what lives in the thinking and practice of our churches. Synod decided:

> 8. That Synod accede to CERCU Recommendation 9: that Synod approve the work of the committee in its reporting of our interaction with the Interchurch Relations Committee of the Free Reformed Churches concerning the Conclusions of Utrecht, that without binding ourselves to any formulations beyond our Confessions, the report gives

faithful expression to what lives in the thinking and practice of our churches (p.71-74).

Grounds:

a. This document accurately reflects what lives among us.

b. Approval of this document would be helpful for the further development of our fraternal relationship as Free Reformed and United Reformed Churches.

c. This document is in accordance with the mandate of CERCU in Phase One, point d., in that it aids in mutual understanding and appreciation of significant factors in the two federations' history, theology, and ecclesiology. Adopted.[1]

Report of the Committee for Ecumenical Relations and Church Unity of the URCNA in Dialogue with the Interchurch Relations Committee of the FRCNA

Some Reflections on the Conclusions of Utrecht

In 1905 the Synod of the Reformed Churches in the Netherlands adopted a testimony concerning 4 doctrinal issues: the order within God's eternal decree (infralapsarianism and supralapsarianism), eternal justification, immediate regeneration, and presumed regeneration (The *Conclusions* of the 1905 Synod are appended in Appendix 2).[2]

Why would the committees of our respective Synods spend time discussing a statement that was adopted by the Reformed Churches in the Netherlands more than a century ago? It is important for our churches to understand that these issues explain, in large measure, the underlying cause for the existence

1. *Acts of Synod Visalia 2014*, Article 26.8.
2. These decisions were taken over by the Christian Reformed Church (CRC) in 1908 as the "Conclusions of Utrecht," and set aside again by the CRC in 1968. The "Conclusions" have no status in the URCNA.

of the Free Reformed Churches in North America today. The issues that led to the adoption of the *Conclusions* in 1905 also play a large role in our history as United Reformed Churches via our roots in the Christian Reformed Church in North America. In 1892, two groups of secession churches in the Netherlands—the 1834 "Afscheiding" or Secession churches and the 1886 "Doleantie" churches—joined together to form the *Gereformeerde Kerken in Nederland* (GKN) or the Reformed Churches in the Netherlands. As a prominent leader in the Doleantie churches, Abraham Kuyper had a strong hand in the ecclesiastical union of 1892. Many among the Afscheiding folk were very concerned about some of Kuyper's doctrinal emphases such as presumed (or assumed) regeneration and justification from eternity. Some of them did not join the church union of 1892, continuing as the *Christelijke Gereformeerde Kerken in Nederland* (CGKN). The Free Reformed Churches in North America trace their roots to this denomination of churches. The major doctrinal differences which separated the CGKN from Abraham Kuyper and his followers resurfaced 13 years later at the Synod of Utrecht where the followers and opponents of Kuyper's distinctive views within the GKN adopted a series of statements which we call the Conclusions of Utrecht.

Because of our historical connections as federations to the issues raised in the *Conclusions*, we agreed as ecumenical committees it would be helpful for the further development of our fraternal relationship as Free Reformed and United Reformed Churches to discuss these matters and present to the churches of both federations our united reflections.

We also ask our respective synods for their approval of the work of the committees in these matters as giving helpful expression to each other as federation of what lives in our churches, with the acknowledgement that we are in no way making binding pronouncements.

Infra- or Supralapsarianism

When God decreed everyone's destiny before the creation of the world, did God first plan man's election or reprobation and then his creation and fall into sin (the supralapsarian position), or did He first plan man's creation and fall, and then his election or reprobation (the infralapsarian position)? The Synod of Utrecht stated that while the Canons of Dort favour the infralapsarian position, both views are acceptable according to Scripture and confession. The Synod added that such profound doctrines which are far beyond the understanding of the common people should be discussed as little as possible in the pulpit.

As committees we would want to add that such profound doctrines are also far beyond the understanding of theologians. We should be careful not to pry into areas of the divine decree which God's Word does not open to us. For this reason the Synod of Dort made no pronouncement on this disputed point. Whatever destiny God has appointed for man, He earnestly and truly declares that all who hear the Gospel of Christ should come to the Christ Whom God has freely and unfeignedly offered to them. In the same way and on His behalf, God calls His Church declare to all persons without distinction the glad tidings of salvation in Jesus Christ to whomever believes (CD II.5; III/IV.8-9).

Eternal Justification

Were all the elect justified before the creation of the world when God chose them in Christ, or are they justified by God when they believe in His Son? The Synod of Utrecht concluded that neither Scripture nor our confessions speak of eternal justification. In the Eternal Counsel of Peace Christ undertook to provide for His people the satisfaction, righteousness and holiness required for their justification. Nevertheless, the Synod said, *it must be maintained with equal firmness that we personally become partakers of this benefit only by a sincere faith.*

As committees we accept this conclusion as Scriptural and confessional. We reject any notion that the elect were justified before the world began, and that by faith they simply become *aware* of their already justified state. This stands opposed to Scripture which teaches that we are the enemies of God and objects of His wrath until through faith in His Son He justifies us. *Having been justified by faith, we have peace with our Lord Jesus Christ* (Rom 5:1). God imputes the righteousness, satisfaction and holiness of Christ to us when we believe in Him. Christ's righteousness becomes ours *in no other way* than by faith *alone* (HC, QA 60,61). Election, Christ's resurrection, and the sacrament of baptism all have something to say about justification, but none of them accomplish it. Thus, in preaching, we call sinners to believe in Jesus Christ and be justified by God.

Immediate or Mediate Regeneration?
In the work of regeneration, does the Holy Spirit always work *mediately*, that is, through the mediation of the Word of God, or does He also on occasion work *immediately*, that is, apart from the Word? It was mainly in relation to the regeneration of infants and the possibility of the salvation of heathen who have never heard the Gospel that the Synod of Utrecht addressed this matter. The Synod judged, in part, that *this regenerating operation of the Holy Spirit should not be in such a way divorced from the preaching of the Word as if these two were separate from each other.* At the same time, the Synod acknowledged the sovereignty of the Holy Spirit as the only Agent of regeneration; the Word and sacraments do not have the power to accomplish this supernatural work.

In our discussion on this point the committees agreed that according to Scripture God is pleased to open the hearts of sinners unto faith by the sovereign power of the Holy Spirit working through and with His Word, both in the Law and the Gospel. On the Day of Pentecost the Spirit pierced many hearts unto salvation through the preaching of the Word. (Acts 2) As Paul preached the Gospel to Lydia the Lord opened her heart to receive God's Word (Acts 16:14-15). The Apostle Peter says that we are *born again of incorruptible seed through the living and enduring Word of God . . . This is the Word that was preached to you* (I Pet 1:23-25).

Our Confessions echo this doctrine of mediate regeneration when we say that Christ effectually calls sinners and draws them into communion with Himself by His Word and Spirit (CD. I.7; cf. H.C. 54). True faith is wrought in man by the hearing of the Word of God and the operation of the Holy Spirit (BC.24, HC 21). Thus, *this supernatural operation of God whereby we are regenerated in no wise excludes or subverts the use of the Gospel which the most wise God has ordained to be the seed of regeneration and food of the soul...Let us not presume to tempt God by separating what He of His good pleasure has intimately joined together* (CD III/IV.17). Even the salvation of infants occurs *by virtue of the covenant of grace* (CD I.17), that is, in connection with the Word of His promise, though the manner is beyond our comprehension. Thus, according to Scripture, hope for regeneration and salvation is found within the context of the presence of God's covenant Word, not beyond.

Presumptive Regeneration
Should we hold that all the children of the covenant are born again and sanctified in Christ until they prove the opposite when they grow up? And should we baptize the children of believers on the grounds that they are already (presumably) regenerated? In answer to the first question, the Synod of Utrecht stated that all children of the covenant *must be held to be regenerated and sanctified in Christ* until they grow up and prove the contrary in doctrine or life. This does not imply that each child is actually born again

since Scripture reveals that they are not all Israel who are of Israel (Rom 9:6-7); it is a judgment of charity made by the Church. Nor does it mean that the time of their rebirth is necessarily prior to their baptism since God fulfills His promise in His own time. Nevertheless, said the Synod, *the sacrament of baptism signifies and seals the washing away of our sins by the blood and the Spirit of Jesus Christ, that is, the justification and the renewal by the Holy Spirit as benefits which God has bestowed upon our seed.*

In the second matter the Synod declared that *it is less correct to say that baptism is to be administered on the ground of their presumed regeneration, since the ground of baptism is found in the command and promise of God.*

In the Free Reformed Churches this particular teaching seems to be the one that engenders greatest concern in their relationship with the United Reformed Churches. Does it live in the midst of the United Reformed Churches in *practice* even though not by *pronouncement*?

As committees we agree that this doctrine goes beyond the bounds of Scripture and therefore does not find a home within our confessions, nor should it find a home in our churches.

First, regarding the *second* matter, we believe that it is *not at all correct* to say that baptism is to be administered on the ground of presumed regeneration, for the Scripture clearly gives us the reason for baptism when it says: *For the promise is to you, and to your children, and to all that are afar off* (Acts 2:38). We echo this teaching when we confess that infants are to be baptized because to them no less than adults are promised the forgiveness of sins through Christ's blood and the Holy Spirit who produces faith (HC, QA 74). By virtue of possessing these promises they are set apart from the world, incorporated into the church, and regarded as covenantally holy, that is, sanctified in Christ (cf. I Cor 7:14; HC, QA 74). Again, in the Belgic Confession of Faith we speak of circumcision and baptism being administered *upon the same promises* (art. 34).

Second, as to the *first* matter, we do not agree that children must be held to be regenerated until they prove otherwise. Scripture teaches that the Holy Spirit can and does at times regenerate infants even in the womb. David trusted the Lord already in his mother's womb (Psalm 71:6; cf. 22:9) and John knew the joy of the Lord before he was born (Luke 1:44). But to say that this is the Holy Spirit's normal operation and that they *must* be held to be regenerate is going beyond Scripture. Such presumption tempts churches and families to neglect the spiritual care of their children in calling them to repent of their sin and to turn to the Lord Jesus Christ in faith. In baptism the Lord seals to us and to our children the promises of forgiveness and eternal life. All the gifts of salvation in Jesus Christ are granted to them in promise. The children must then be led to the Lord through diligent instruction and called to take hold of what has been promised to them in Christ. As they, by the power of the Spirit, embrace Christ in true faith, the Holy Spirit will impart to them what they have in Christ, namely, the washing away of sins and newness of life. Through faith they will demonstrate the new life in the way of putting off sin and putting on Christ (cf. Form for the Baptism of Infants).

Appendix 2: The Conclusions of Utrecht 1905

Synod of Utrecht 1905, translated by J. Mark Beach

As for the first point[1], which has to do with *infra-* and *supralapsarianism*, Synod declares

- that, certainly with respect to the doctrine of election, our Confessional standards follow the infralapsarian presentation, but, as is evident both from the wording of Head I, Article 7, of the *Canons of Dort* and from the deliberations at the Synod of Dort, it is by no means intended that the supralapsarian interpretation is thereby excluded or condemned;

- that, accordingly, on the one hand, it is not right to present the supralapsarian view as being properly *the* doctrine of the Reformed churches in the Netherlands, nor on the other hand to harass anyone who has accepted the supralapsarian interpretation for himself,

1. This translation was made by Dr. J. Mark Beach of Mid-America Reformed Seminary and is used with his permission. For an earlier translation see the *Acts of Synod 1942 of the Christian Reformed Church*, Supplement XVII (pp. 352–4).

since the Synod of Dort did not make a decision regarding this disputed point.

To this the Synod adds the warning

- that such profound doctrines (which are beyond the comprehension of common people) should be brought to the pulpit as little as possible, and that one should adhere to the presentation given in our Confessional standards in the preaching of the Word and in catechetical instruction.

Concerning the second point, *eternal justification*, Synod declares

- that this expression itself does not occur in our Confessions, but that on that account it may not be disapproved, any more than the expression "covenant of works," and such like, which are simply theological terms;

- that it is incorrect to say that our Confessions know only of a justification by and through faith, seeing that both the Word of God in Romans 4:25 and our Confession in Article 20 emphatically speak of an objective justification sealed in the resurrection of Christ, which, in temporal sequence, precedes subjective justification;

- that, as far as the matter itself is concerned, all our churches heartily believe and confess that Christ from eternity, in the counsel of peace, has given himself as surety for his people, and has taken their guilt upon himself, just as afterward, through his suffering and death on Calvary, he actually paid the ransom for us and reconciled us to God while we were yet enemies, but that it must be maintained just as definitely, on the basis of the Word of God and in agreement with our Confessional standards, that we personally become partakers of this benefit only by true faith.

For which reason the Synod earnestly warns against

- any presentation of the matter which detracts from either the eternal suretyship of Christ for his elect or the demand of true faith to be justified before the righteousness of God in the tribunal of conscience.

In regard to the third point, that of *immediate regeneration*, Synod declares

- that this expression can be used in a good sense, insofar as our churches have always confessed, over against the Lutherans and the Roman Catholic church, that regeneration is not effected through the Word or the Sacraments as such, but through the almighty and regenerating work of the Holy Spirit;

- that this regenerating work of the Holy Spirit, however, may not in that sense be divorced from the preaching of the Word, as if both were separated from each other; for, although our Confession teaches that we need not be in doubt respecting the salvation of our children who die in infancy though they have not heard the preaching of the gospel, and our Confessional standards nowhere express themselves as to the manner in which regeneration is effected in the case of these and other children—yet, on the other hand, it is certain that the gospel is a power of God unto salvation for every one who believes, and that in the case of adults the regenerating work of the Holy Spirit accompanies the preaching of the gospel.

Although Synod does not doubt that God is also powerfully able, even among the heathen, to regenerate those whom he wills without the preaching of the Word, yet Synod judges on the basis of God's Word

- that we can make no pronouncement regarding the question whether this actually happens, and that therefore we must adhere to the rule that the revealed Word gives to us, and leave the hidden things to the Lord our God.

Finally, regarding the fourth point, that of *assumed regeneration* (*onderstelde wedergeboorte*), Synod declares

- that, according to the Confession of our churches, the seed of the covenant must, in virtue of the promise of God, be regarded as regenerated and sanctified in Christ, until, as they grow up, the contrary is evident from their life or doctrine;

- that, however, it is less correct to say that baptism is administered to believers' children on the ground of their assumed (*onderstelde*) regeneration, for the ground of baptism is the command and promise of God;

- that furthermore, the judgment of charity, whereby the church regards the seed of the covenant as regenerated, does not therefore in any way imply that every child is truly regenerated, since God's Word teaches us that not all are Israel who are from Israel, and regarding Isaac it is said: "in him shall your seed be named" (Rom. 9:6, 7), so that in preaching, serious self-examination shall be urged continually, inasmuch as only those who believe and are baptized shall be saved.

Furthermore Synod maintains, together with our Confession,

- that the sacraments "are not empty and hollow signs to deceive us," but "are visisble signs and seals of something internal and invisible, by means of which God works in us through the power of the Holy Spirit" (Article 33), and that in particular baptism is called "the washing of regeneration" and "the washing away of sins" because God wants "to assure us by this divine pledge and sign that we are as truly cleansed from our sins spiritually as we are physically washed with water"; for which reason, in the prayer after baptism, our church thanks and praises God that he has forgiven us and our children all our sins, through the blood of his beloved Son Jesus Christ, and received us through the his Holy Spirit to be his children, and sealed and confirmed this to us by holy baptism; so that our Confessional standards clearly teach that the sacrament of baptism signifies and seals the washing away of sins by the blood and Spirit of Jesus Christ, that is, justification and renewal by the Holy Spirit as benefits that God has bestowed upon our seed.

Meanwhile Synod is of the opinion that the representation that every elect child is therefore already in fact regenerated before being baptized, cannot be proved either on the basis of Scripture or on the basis of the Confession, since God sovereignly fulfills his promise in his own time, whether before, during, or after baptism, so that one is required to exercise caution in this regard and not want to be wise above what God has revealed to us.

From the *Acts of the General Synod of the Reformed Churches in the Netherlands*, held at Utrecht (1905), Art. 158.

Indices

Adam
  faith, trust of Adam, 26
  freedom of choice, 24, 45
  goal or end of Adam's
    obedience, 99, 104
  "justification" of Adam, 14–15,
    26
  merit of Adam, 14–15, 26
  mutable fellowship, 25
  obedience of Adam, 14–15, 26
    supplied by Christ, 63
  possible instability pre-fall,
    45
  probationary command, 42
Barthianism, 50,
Bavinck, Herman, 6, 15, 53, 111
Berkhof, Louis, 32 n.5, 53
Calvin, John, 15
CanRC (Canadian Reformed
  Churches)
  covenant theology too
    exclusive? 49
  practice of Lord's Supper,
    77–78
  role of the Canons of Dort in
    CanRCs, 70–71
  role of practical issues in
    church unity, 84
  CanRCs and piety, 87–91
CCU (Committee for Church
  Unity, CanRC)
CERCU (Committee for
  Ecumenical Relations and
  Church Unity, URCNA)
Children in the covenant of
  grace, 80–81, 87–91, 107,
  122, 126–27
Christ
  active and passive obedience,
    15, 56, 60
    related to two natures,
      62–63
  imputation of active
    obedience (aka IAOC),
    27–28, 56, 57–58, 60

merits of Christ, 28
as second/last Adam, 42,
    61–63
covenant theology intended
    to glorify Christ, 93–94
Christians, marks of, 19
Church
    militant and triumphant, 75
    visible and invisible, 18, 34,
        54–55
    pluriformity, 54
Church unity, 2–3
    positive conclusions 40, 64,
        66, 100, 107, 112
    postpone indefinitely, 9,
        112–113
Communal vs. personal, 6, 49
Conclusions of Utrecht, 10,
    115–127
Confessions of Faith
    limits of confessions, 23, 104
    relation to Scripture, 62
    relation to theological
        constructions, 76, 104
Covenant
    assurance of God's promises,
        17
    blessings, 16
    breaking the covenant, 16
    covenant and baptism, 31
    covenant and election (see
        also election), 30–31, 33,
        43, 47–48, 56–57, 58
    covenant and preaching,
        81–82, 100
    covenant of grace, 16–18,
        30–33
        saving efficacy vs.
            historical
            administration
            ("dual aspect"), 17,
            30–32, 44, 54
        as instrument of
            salvation, 17
        properly a second
            covenant, 17–18
    covenant of redemption/
        peace, 69–72
    covenant of works (pre-fall
        covenant), 14–16, 24–30,
        41–2, 63
        terms to describe, 26,
            29, 111
    demands/obligations of the
        covenant, 16, 32–33
    living in the covenant, 32,
        100
    Mosaic covenant, 72–74
    promises of the covenant,
        promise and obligation,
        16, 32–33, 58, 81–82
    threats of the covenant, 16
Election, elect, chosen, 17
    and assurance, 17
    in Christ, 17
Faith

faith and works, 59
faith as instrument of
　justification, 18, 59, 111
Federal Vision, 4, 55–57, 58–59,
　86, 110
Genevan tunes for the Psalms,
　37, 46
Hesselink, I. John, 106
Hypocrisy, hypocrites, 32,
　33–34, 55, 100, 106
Infra- or Supralapsarianism,
　118
Justification, 14
　distinguished from
　　sanctification, 33, 58–60
　defended in two possible
　　ways, 61, 110
　eternal justification, 118–119,
　　124–25
Kuyper, Abraham, 117
Law and Gospel, 15, 28, 58–59,
　65, 74, 99
　uses of the law, 73, 106
　gospel to be "obeyed," 28,
　　74–76, 99, 104–106
　wider and narrower senses of
　　"law," 106
Liberation of 1944, 4, 34, 48, 50,
　52–53, 85, 86
Liturgical forms, 7, 28, 32, 58,
　80, 81, 107, 122
Objective vs. subjective, 6, 49,
　52

OPC (Orthodox Presbyterian
　Church), 22, 66
Pactum salutis—see covenant of
　redemption
Pelagian errors, 29, 97
Posse peccare, etc., 25, esp. 25n.1,
　30, 44–46, 63
Reformed Baptists, 73–74
Reformed Scholastics, 8, 50, 70
Regeneration
　mediate or immediate?
　　119–120, 125–26
　presumed regeneration, 10,
　　52, 120–22, 126–27
Republication of the covenant
　of works, 72–73
Schilder, Klaas; Schilderite, 32
　n.5, 53, 48, 53, 55, 59–60, 75,
　111
Sin
　fall into sin, 15, 16, 25, 45, 97,
　　118
　sin and the believer, 78–79
Strange, Alan, 9
Synods, CanRC
　Fergus 1998, 22
　Neerlandia 2001, 3
　Carman 2013, 84
　Synod of Dort (1618–1619), 27,
　　34, 51
Synods, URCNA
　Escondido 2001, 3
　Schererville 2007, 4, 86

London 2010, 4, 86
Visalia 2014, 96
Turretin, Francis, 18 n.1, 27, 48
URCNA (United Reformed Churches of North America)
    more presbyterianized in USA, 6, 49–50, 51–52, 110
    Pastoral Advice and *Doctrinal Affirmations*, 4, 85
Ursinus, Zacharias, 99
Vos, Geerhardus, 23, 32 n.5

Scripture references
Gen 1:31, 25
Gen 2:17, 25, 29, 45
Gen 3:8, 25
Gen 3:17, 14, 42
Gen 3:22, 25
Gen 15:12–21, 46–47
Gen 15:18, 30
Gen 17:4, 32
Deut 7:9, 15
Deut 29:1, 9–14, 31
Isa 49, 70
Jer 31:32, 32
Psalm 19, 105
Psalm 71:6, 122
Psalm 22:9, 122
Psalm 119, 28, 105
Matt 7:21, 11:30, 105
Luke 1:44, 122
Luke 24:27, 93

John 1:17, 15
John 3:36, 28, 99, 106
John 5:39, 93
John 6:29, 93
John 17:4, 93
John 12:21, 8, 93
John 17:20–21, 113
Acts 2:38, 121
Acts 16:14–15, 120
Rom 2:28–29, 32
Rom 4:15, 15
Rom 5:1, 119
Rom 5:12–21, 15
Rom 5:18, 63
Rom 7:12, 14, 16, 22, 25, 105
Rom 8:1–4, 105
Rom 8:7–8, 45
Rom 9:1ff., 23
Rom 9:6–13, 30
Rom 9:6–8, 19, 121
Rom 10:16, 104
Rom 15:18–19, 105
1 Cor 1:30, 93
1 Cor 2:2, 93
1 Cor 4:7, 27
1 Cor 7:14, 121
1 Cor 9:21, 28, 105
2 Cor 3:6, 15
2 Cor 5:20, 105
2 Cor 6:14–7:1, 76, 105
2 Cor 9:13, 105
Gal 3:7–14, 31
Gal 3:15–18, 31

Gal 3:19, 15
Gal 5:13–15, 105
Gal 6:2, 28, 105
Eph 1, 70
Eph 1:4, 30
Eph 4:1–3, 113
Eph 5:22–33, 32
Eph 6:2–3, 28
1 Thess 2:13, 76
2 Thess 1:8, 28, 75, 99
1 Tim 1:8–11, 106
2 Tim 1:10, 93, 105
2 Tim 2:19, 18
Titus 2:1, 105
Heb 6:4–8, 106
Heb 10:28–29, 12:25, 105
1 Pet 1:23–25, 120
1 Pet 2:8, 3:1, 4:17, 104
Rev 3:14–22, 76, 99, 105
Rev 21, 46
Rev 21–22, 25

Confessions of Faith
Belgic Confession articles
  art. 14, 14, 16
  art. 20–24, 15–16
  art. 22, 27
  art. 24, 33, 120
  art. 29, 18–19, 33–35, 55
  art. 34, 31, 122
  Canons of Dort chapters and articles
  all, 33

1, art. 7, 63, 120
1, art. 17, 31, 111, 120, 123
2 all, 16
2, art. 1–4, 62
2, art. 5, 100
2, art. 8, 17
2, rej. errors, 17, 43, 111
3/4, art. 2, 16
3/4, art. 17, 120
5, art. 14, 28, 76, 99
Heidelberg Catechism Lord's Days
LD 2–7, 15
LD 2, 15
LD 3–6, 16
LD 3, 14, 26, 98–99
LD 6, 63
LD 7, 111
LD 15–17, 16
LD 16, 14–15
LD 21, 15, 120
LD 23–24, 15, 16, 27, 33, 61, 111, 119
LD 27, 31, 121
LD 32, 61, 106
LD 33, 106, 111
LD 44, 15, 106
Westminster Confession and Catechisms
WCF 7.2, 26
WLC 20, 26

About the Authors

Dr. J. Mark Beach (Ph.D., Calvin) serves as professor of ministerial and doctrinal studies at Mid-America Reformed Seminary in Dyer, IN (he belongs to the URCNA).

Rev. John A. Bouwers (M.Div.) serves as pastor of Immanuel United Reformed Church in Jordan, ON (since 1992).

Dr. Robert P. Godfrey (Ph.D., Stanford) serves as professor of church history and president of Westminster Seminary California (he belongs to the URCNA).

Rev. Daniel R. Hyde (M.Div., Th.M.) serves as pastor of Oceanside United Reformed Church in Oceanside, CA (since 2000).

Dr. Theodore G. Van Raalte (Ph.D., Calvin) serves as professor of ecclesiology at the Canadian Reformed Theological Seminary in Hamilton, ON (he belongs to the CanRC).

Dr. Jason P. Van Vliet (Th.D., Apeldoorn) serves as professor of dogmatics at the Canadian Reformed Theological Seminary in Hamilton, ON (he belongs to the CanRC).

Dr. Cornelis P. Venema (Ph.D., Princeton) serves as professor of doctrinal studies and president of Mid-America Reformed Seminary in Dyer, IN (he belongs to the URCNA).

www.ingramcontent.com/pod-product-compliance
Lightning Source LLC
Chambersburg PA
CBHW072048290426
44110CB00014B/1591